W9-AEC-782

SIX FACES OF COURAGE

SIX FACES OF COURAGE

Secret agents against Nazi tyranny

by

M.R.D. FOOT

with a preface by
R.V. Jones

LEO COOPER

First published in Great Britain in 1978 by
Eyre Methuen Ltd
Reprinted by Magnum 1980

This revised and updated edition published in 2003 by
LEO COOPER
an imprint of Pen & Sword Books,
47 Church Street,
Barnsley
South Yorkshire,
S70 2AS

ISBN 0 85052 965 4

A catalogue record for this book is
available from the British Library.

Typeset in 11/14pt Sabon by
Phoenix Typesetting, Burley-in-Wharfedale, West Yorkshire.

Printed in England by
CPI UK

Contents

Preface

If courage is, as Winston Churchill has said, 'the quality that guarantees all others', it also takes many forms. For Lord Moran, in *The Anatomy of Courage*, it was the kind brought out by the desperate battles of the Flanders trenches. And, for Robert Graves, not only in feats of action. In *Goodbye to All That* he describes how a fellow officer, Captain A.L. Samson of the Royal Welch Fusiliers, fell mortally wounded and groaning some twenty yards out from the front line. He was so respected that three men were killed and another four wounded in trying to get him back. His own orderly reached him, but Samson sent him back with an apology for making so much noise, and then went silent. When at dusk Graves found him he was dead, hit in seventeen places and with his knuckles forced into his mouth to stop himself crying out and attracting any more men to their death. Such exemplary courage is not confined to the battlefield – I have seen the same spirit in an elderly woman, irremediably bedridden for years with an unmending thigh bone so broken that the end projected to her skin, and bearing it un-complainingly so as to be less burden to those around her.

Few men have spoken of courage with such understanding as Lord Slim. In a 1946 broadcast, he remarked that environment was important: 'It is the lands where nature is neither too easy nor too cruel, where a man must work hard to live but where his efforts and enterprise can bring him great rewards, that breed courage and where it becomes a natural tradition. And don't run away with the idea that this limits courage to northern Europe and North

America. Believe me – and I've fought both with them and against them – some of the bravest races in the world aren't white at all.' Again, Winston Churchill, contemplating the Dervish dead after Omdurman wrote: '. . . yet these were as brave men as ever walked the earth . . . destroyed, not conquered, by machinery.' And since we remember with horror the atrocities committed by the Germans, let us recall that their fighting men were not without courage. When the *Tirpitz* was capsized by our bombers, the doomed men trapped inside the hull were heard singing 'Deutschland über Alles'.

Lord Slim movingly emphasized that courage in battle is only one form: '. . . the fighting man is the last to claim a monopoly in courage . . . In the retreat in Burma in 1942, I was deeply proud of the troops . . . Yet the outstanding impression of courage I carried away from that desperate campaign was from the Indian women refugees. Day after day, mile after mile, they plodded on, through dust or mud, their babies in their arms, children clinging to their skirts, harried by ruthless enemies, strafed from the air, shelterless, caught between the lines in every battle, yet patient and un-complaining, devoted, thinking only of their families – so very brave.'

Beyond physical courage lies moral courage – and it would be hard to disagree with Lord Slim's observation that this is much the rarer. How often, for example, do we see a political leader risking his future as Robert Peel did when – as Prime Minister – he turned against his party to repeal the Corn Laws: 'To incur the heaviest responsibility . . . and to be at the same time the tool of a party – that is to say, to adopt the opinions of men who have not access to your knowledge and could not profit by it if they had . . . would be an odious servitude to which I never would submit.'

But if we can immediately recognize moral courage when we encounter it at any political level from the village Hampden up to Robert Peel, some of its manifestations are less obvious. I have in mind, for example, the courage of those theoretical physicists who stood by their calculations that the exploding of a thermonuclear bomb would not start a reaction that would burn up all the hydrogen in the oceans and thus exterminate humanity.

The courage of which Professor Foot writes with such understanding and warmth is the kind brought out by the Resistance movements against the Nazis in the Second World War and he has taken six examples. Of these, four (Jean Moulin and Marie-Madeleine Fourcade in France, Andrée de Jongh in Belgium and Witold Pilecki in Poland) were in their own countries when they were overrun by the Germans, and they must first have had to face the agonizing moral decision of whether to stay or whether to escape in the hope of continuing the fight from outside. Has any great playwright, incidentally, debated such a situation? The other two (Harry Peulevé and Victor Gerson, respectively of French and Jewish extraction) were of British nationality; Peulevé a television cameraman at Alexandra Palace and Gerson a dealer in fine rugs in Paris who escaped to England during the German advance in France.

Their operations were of very different kinds, and illustrate the different forms that resistance can take. It is this that justifies Professor Foot's title *Six Faces of Courage*, for his six figures really have much in common in the courage they exhibit, which was called forth by circumstances different from any that I have cited earlier, a distinguishing feature being the isolation in which resistance workers had to operate. This was part of the price that they had to pay for whatever degree of security they could achieve in a treacherous environment. Only rarely did they know, for example, whether the information that they had obtained at great risk could find its way back to London and whether we would act upon it. I warmly recall a day in 1942 when I read on a badly focused microfilm a report of some Belgian agents about the German nightfighter radar stations in their area. After mentioning that in reconnoitring one station in their area they had been shot at by a sentry 'fortunately with more zeal than accuracy', they concluded:

As far as our work is concerned, it would be helpful if we knew to what extent you and the British services are interested. We have been working so long in the dark that any reaction from London about our work could be welcome to such obscure workers as ourselves. We hope that you will not take this in bad part since, whatever may happen, you can rely on our entire devotion and on the sacrifice of our lives.

Fortunately in this particular case we were shortly able to give them tangible evidence that their work was not in vain by bombing the local nightfighter headquarters, and later by the dropping of 'Window' to confuse the radars. But there must have been far too many other instances where there was no visible response to acts of the greatest gallantry, and where men and women died without ever knowing whether their sacrifice had been worthwhile.

There were primarily three aspects of resistance: the obtaining of intelligence, the assisting of Allied servicemen escaping from enemy-held territory, and the sabotage of German installations and resources. My own concern was primarily with intelligence and my closest connection with any of Professor Foot's six examples was with the incredibly brave Marie-Madeleine Fourcade. Hers is a magnificent story which she herself has told admirably in *Noah's Ark*. In it she reproduces a copy of a report that was forwarded by her organization to us in London in August 1943, which told us about the organization that the Germans were setting up for the V-bombardment of London ten months later. It contained so much inner detail concerning the organization (such as the regimental designation and the commanding officer's name, and the kinds of passes needed for entry to Peenemünde) that I immediately asked who the source was, but all that Marie-Madeleine could tell me was that it was 'Une jeune fille la plus remarquable de sa génération.' After the war, I learnt her name: she was Jeannie Rousseau, known to her network as 'Amniarix', and equally brave with Marie-Madeleine. At the time of her report she was twenty-three years old, and had been working for the Resistance since she was twenty. Youth was indeed a feature common to many resistance workers, although some, of course, were of maturer years, such as Jean Moulin and Witold Pilecki. Marie-Madeleine herself, at the head of an organization of between 2,000 and 3,000 workers was only thirty and Dedée de Jongh, whose famous 'Comet' escape line brought out seven hundred Allied airmen, was in her mid-twenties.

Another characteristic of resistance workers was how readily they would sacrifice themselves for others. The head of Jeannie Rousseau's network 'les Druides' was a former University friend, Georges Lamarque, again little older than she was. Ultimately traced by the Germans to a particular village by his radio transmissions, he gave himself up in order to save the village from savagery, and was summarily executed. Jeannie herself was captured with two companions after D-Day in 1944, just as they were about to board a boat to England from Brittany. She had left them in a car when the Gestapo caught her and made her walk back to the car with them. One can guess at the fears running through her mind during those minutes: at best a concentration camp: at worst . . . ? But even in that dire situation she thought of the others, and talked loudly in German to her captors to give her companions a chance to escape. One got away: the other, Yves le Bitoux, realized that they were in his home town, and the Germans might wreak vengeance on it if he were to escape, and he therefore allowed himself to be taken. He died in a concentration camp. Jeannie Rousseau was sent not to one concentration camp, but three in turn – Ravensbrück, Torgau and Königsberg. She survived; but hundreds of Marie-Madeleine's agents, both men and women, were murdered before the war ended.

Thirty-three years after her dramatic report, I met Jeannie Rousseau, now Vicomtesse de Clarens. She wrote a gracious foreword to my own book and her words vividly portray those characteristics of resistance work which to my mind call for the utmost in courage:

Some of us were told to collect pedestrian facts; others were given specific instructions; others still were asked to keep ears and eyes open for the unusual, the improbable; all were working in small, compartmented fields in almost complete isolation – the price to pay for lessening danger – and yet saw friend after friend, comrade after comrade fall into the ever gaping trap.

It is not easy to depict the lonesomeness, the chilling fear, the unending waiting, the frustration of not knowing whether the dangerously obtained information would be passed on – or passed on in time – or recognized as vital in the maze of the 'couriers'.

Courage in battle is at least helped by the presence of others, and perhaps by the fear of shaming oneself in front of them; and it may well be summoned by the sight of a comrade in need of rescue. But resistance men and women were for much of the time alone with their fears, often in the hands of their perverted enemies. That is when character is most severely tested and we who have not ex-perienced it can only imagine how great the strain can be.

An example that brought the difference home to me occurred in 1950, when I was concerned with safety in coal-mines, and some Scottish miners were trapped when the roof of their Knockshinoch colliery collapsed. Fortunately, their telephone line to the surface survived. Entombed for days, they kept calm, and when, against all the odds, they were ultimately rescued, they testified to the effect of the telephone contact with the surface in maintaining their morale. And in the 'We have a problem' Apollo mission breakdown, the magnificent bearing of the spacecraft crew was supported throughout by radio contact with base. For lone resistance workers, no such support was possible: through long periods of intense strain they had only the support of their own characters and belief in the cause they served.

In looking for the feature common to the six individuals of whom he writes, Professor Foot singles out one quality: integrity. Lord Moran said almost the same thing: 'I contend that fortitude in war has its roots in morality; that selection is a search for character, and that war itself is but one more test – the supreme and final test if you will – of character.' And while Lord Moran was speaking of the battlefield, I would say that – for the reasons I have given – resist-ance work is an even more supreme and final test. And that is why those of us who were privileged to know men and women of the Resistance write of them with such unanimous admiration.

R.V. Jones

Author's Note to new edition

While writing in the mid-1970s a survey of resistance to Nazism in occupied Europe, I kept having to dismiss in a few sentences, or even to leave out altogether, individuals of quite astonishing capacity and courage. This book sets out to repair, in half a dozen cases, these omissions. This revised version brings all six studies up to date, removing some inaccuracies in the earlier version and referring the reader to some fresh sources for further study.

I chose to write about these six people in particular because their strength, endurance, and delight in originality are qualities that are worth recall in an age less heroic than theirs. For every one of the half-dozen, hundreds more can be found who equalled them in bravery; few, if any, who surpassed them.

I remain greatly indebted, for conversations and correspondence at various times, and for leave to publish copyright material, including photographs, to Vera Atkins, Kenneth Cohen, Marie-Madeleine Fourcade, Joseph Garliński, Victor Gerson, Martin Heller, Leslie Humphreys, Selwyn Jepson, Andrée de Jongh, Jimmy Langley, Henri Michel, Laure Moulin, Airey Neave, Gilbert Renault-Roulier and Annette Weston, and trust that, in a work of history, they and their shades and relatives – almost all of them, alas, are now dead – will none of them mind being mentioned by name without distinction of rank or title. I am indebted also to the Controller, HMSO, for leave to reproduce a passage in Crown copyright.

Acknowledgements and thanks are due also to the Comité

d'Histoire de la Deuxième Guerre Mondiale for the photograph of Jean Moulin and to the Librairie Académique Perrin for that of Andrée de Jongh.

Unattributed translations are my own, as are any remaining errors.

Nuthampstead   M.R.D.F.
14 December 2002

1

Resisters and resistance movements

As the great war of 1939–45, the second of last century's world wars, recedes in time, its shape in history becomes more clear. People get less obsessed with the fate of their own family, their own province, their own country, and are more ready to take notice of what happened to other people in other places. It is plain already that within this world war there were really two big wars in parallel: the struggle with Nazi Germany – which from the Germans' point of view was the Nazis' struggle for world supremacy – and the struggle with the Japanese, who tried to set up by force their own 'Greater East Asia Co-Prosperity Sphere'.

Mixed in with these two great contests between great powers, there were several other wars. For example, the Spanish Civil War of 1936–9, a sort of dress rehearsal for the impending conflict for mastery in Europe; the Russo-Finnish Winter War of 1939–40; the Yugoslav Civil War of 1941–6 and the Chinese Civil War of 1934–49. In Palestine and Vietnam, among many other colonies, the early forties saw the preparatory stages of wars of national liberation, in which the main fighting still lay ahead in the winter of 1944–5, when Weizmann, the creator of modern Israel, was expressing 'deep moral indignation and horror' at Lord Moyne's murder by Jewish gunmen[1] (one of them later Prime Minister of Israel), and Ho Chi Minh's life was about to be saved by American secret service doctors.[2]

None of these wars was decided, as most earlier wars had been, by the efforts of uniformed armed forces alone. Since the United

1

States' Civil War of 1861–5 and the German Civil War of 1866, the seven weeks' war between Prussia and Austria, the impact of railways on war had been marked, and the World War of 1914–18 had also shown the strategic weight of industrial power, which weighed in heavily again next time. Moreover, the next World War saw activity almost everywhere, in territories overrun by the fighting, by a combatant force that had not had much chance to act in 1914–18: resistance.

The 1914 war's proximate cause was a Serb student's act of resistance, the assassination at Sarajevo. The next four years of fighting scoured out the Balkans too thoroughly for much clandestine work there to be conceivable. In the wastes of eastern Europe there was some guerilla activity of an unorganized kind – not much more than banditry – which became more serious during the Russian Civil War of 1917–20 until it was cleaned up by Trotsky's Red Army. The Easter Rising in Dublin in 1916 was a dismal failure at the time, but was so clumsily put down that it had a posthumous success: the Irish republic of today claims to date back to it. The Rising was an act of resistance if ever there was one, presaging the Troubles of 1919–22 and since 1969; items in the secular struggle between Ireland and England that has raged since the twelfth century and is far from over today (a distant bomb resounded as this paragraph was being revised in north London in 1977).

The main resistance movement in 1914–18, the Arab revolt against the Turks, became world-famous, and had a perceptible impact on the course of the war. This revolt, guided in part by the genius of T. E. Lawrence, liberated the Arabian peninsula and helped British imperial troops to conquer Mesopotamia and the Levant coast from Gaza to Alexandretta, with results a lot less satisfying politically to the Arabs than they or Lawrence had hoped. Lawrence has left a tremendous legend, and wrote a tremendous book, *Seven Pillars of Wisdom*;[3] in an even less heroic age than his, thousands of young men hoped they could imitate him.

During the wars of 1939–45 no new Lawrence appeared, nobody having quite the combination of brain, daring, eccentricity, opportunity and luck. There might have been an opportunity in China, had the Chinese not thrown up Mao Tse-tung and Chou En-lai, who read Lawrence, approved – indeed, took up – his doctrine of irregular warfare, and were far from sharing his hatred of politics. And in Europe too there was local talent enough to lead resistance; none of the brilliant strangers sent in from America, Britain or Russia to help were able to work Lawrence's magic. Instead a few produced some passable imitations of Robert Jordan, the hero of Ernest Hemingway's *For Whom the Bell Tolls*.[4]

All over Nazi- and Fascist-occupied Europe there was resistance to the fact of occupation. Outside the two home countries of Germany and Italy, this took several forms, usually including armed insurrection, and many Italian opponents of Fascism, who had had to lie low while Mussolini held real power, made up for time lost and ran a vigorous partisan movement in the last twenty months of the war. In occupied France, Norway, Denmark, the Low Countries, in truncated Czechoslovakia, in re-partitioned Poland; all over the Balkans; the whole population outside the resistance movements became aware that there were resisters around and among them. In all these countries it took only a few years of Nazi occupation for most people to decide that they wanted the Nazis to go. Even in the Baltic states, which had been independent from 1918 till the USSR annexed them in 1940 and had strong local traditions of anti-semitism, even in the western republics of the USSR itself, which the Germans had overrun, republics that had lived under communist dictatorship since communism seized power in 1917; almost everyone came to agree that a Nazi German regime was the worst of all possible systems, and must end.

The official historians – except for the handful of us who write about SOE – all say that Nazi Germany was beaten by the combined armed forces, the soldiers, sailors and airmen, of the powers allied against it: principally, the USA, the USSR and the United Kingdom. People who came under Nazi occupation know this, and are grateful for it, but they know too that there was a fourth force at work besides the armies, the navies and the air forces: the resisters, supported by and drawn from the common people of occupied territory. As a rule resisters worked in parallel

3

harness with the rest. Some of them were so wholly independent-minded that they could not work closely with anybody; they suffered the usual fate of cranks, disappointment. Some of the others got so completely involved in their countries' politics during the anti-Nazi struggle that post-war history is unintelligible without them: de Gaulle and Tito are the outstanding examples. Parri and Togliatti in Italy, Damaskinos in Greece, Lie the first secretary of the United Nations, King Haakon of Norway, Queen Wilhelmina of the Netherlands provide other, if not quite so familiar, instances. Resisters were an infinitely varied lot; not many generalizations can apply to them.

One or two can be ventured, all the same. They shared one aim in Europe, at least after 22 June 1941 – the day the German attack on the USSR began: that aim was to get rid of German Nazi occupation. And they shared one characteristic besides bravery: contrariness. They were disputatious, argumentative, non-conformist, did not enjoy being ordered about. An unusually high proportion of them were women, well before some of their daughters got going in the women's liberation movements of today. And they all, without exception, tried to be brave, even though when it came to the point of danger some turned out arrant cowards.[5]

The first, indispensable task for a resister was to make an act of will: to form a private, unshakeable determination that the Germans must go. 'He that wills the end, will the means'; yet means and opportunity had to fit together. Each country had its own systems, methods, favoured forms of organization. Some were more easily reached by particular great powers than others; for instance, the nearness of the Red Army with its penchant for partisans gave a distinctive flavour to resistance in eastern Europe. Distance, or proximity, could not help affecting the course, the scale and the kind of each resistance struggle.

There was much talk in the 1950s and 60s of the European resistance struggle, but the truth is that none existed on a continental scale. The communist-dominated partisan movements were all infused with similar doctrines, including enthusiasm for 'our gallant Soviet ally'; without whose sublime efforts the rest of the continent

4

would indeed probably have gone under. The paradox of freedom being saved by an unfree state is odd, but need not blind us to the points at issue, which are two. The partisan movements, though usually important, nowhere constituted the whole of the resistance effort, and this effort was everywhere organized on a local or a national and not on a supranational or European basis.

Many people hated the Nazis, and longed to see them depart, but never found a chance to do anything about sending them packing. Others had more insight or more luck. Leo Baeck, for an eminent example, a leading rabbi in Germany in the thirties, would not flee from the Nazi menace, and could not believe it was wholly evil. He was arrested in 1943 and put in the concentration camp of Theresienstadt, and there used to lecture, most evenings, quietly, to anybody who would come to listen. He discussed the philosophical doctrines of Plato and Aristotle, or recited the great Greek classic dramas, which he knew by heart, in his own German translation. This, in a punishment camp run by the death's head division of the SS, was an individual act that ran counter to the whole system of Nazi dictatorship; though unarmed, it was a significant act of resistance and of courage. When the camp was liberated, the former prisoners proposed to lynch their guards. Baeck gently remarked that it would be more just to put them on trial, and had a personality strong enough to impose his humane impulse even on that starving and exasperated mob.

Few people have such strength of personality, or so keen a sense of what is due to law, and few people have Baeck's intellect or his bravery. Only at that level of austere originality could resisters make much impact as individuals. As a rule they had to form into groups, to exercise any real effect, and in spite of working against the cult of leadership that was one of the central doctrines of Fascism and Nazism, they needed to have leaders themselves. Resistance leaders were not worshipped by crowds numbering scores of thousands, chanting *Sieg Heil, Sieg Heil* or *Duce Duce*; their smaller followings were no less devoted than Hitler's and Mussolini's, but behaved in a more modest way. Leaders were indispensable: leading from in front at the rare moments of action, providing guidance, understanding of wider issues, hope, a broader view, in the quieter but hardly less dangerous spells in between.

Besides, it was a good deal safer for groups of resisters to deal with other groups, or with outside authorities, through a single channel than through several. Never multiply risks was a vital resisters' rule; not always followed even by the best of them. When, for instance, one of the first V-1 pilotless buzz-bombs ever fired, for testing purposes in the Baltic, accidentally went off course and crash-landed (without exploding) on the Danish island of Bornholm, some quick-witted Danes photographed the wreckage before the Germans got to it. The photographs were passed to a network of spies in Copenhagen, senior men who were in touch with London. They thought them so important that they forwarded several copies, through separate channels; one at least of their less experienced messengers was caught.[6] London got the material all right, but so did Berlin. All the photographers were arrested; they seized an heroic occasion to keep silent.

The history of resistance, everywhere, is cram full of incidents like this: blind folly and blind heroism marching in step. Before we get too deep in narrative or obsessed by anecdote, we need to spell out resisters' tasks more carefully. What sorts of work could they do to lessen the Germans' hold on their countries? Wishing alone is never strong enough to get rid of a secret policeman.

There were three kinds of work that could affect the course of the occupation and of the war: work for military intelligence, work in hiding other people and helping them to escape, and work on sub-version. Subversion in turn could be of several kinds, ranging through rumour-spreading and other kinds of propaganda – such as the distributing of leaflets and illegal newspapers – to minor and major sabotage, and from minor attacks on troops to full-blooded insurrection. Of each of these three main categories, intelligence, escape and subversion, a little more needs to be said.

The occupied peoples could not rely on getting rid of the Nazis by themselves, they were much too weak. In every occupied state, the first thing everyone had to realize was how very much too weak they had just been proved to be, by the fact of defeat. Even in a state as strong – potentially – as the USSR, nothing like enough had been done in time to make that potential strength actual, before the Germans struck. So the occupied had to look to those who were still free of the Nazis, to the main Russian, British and American forces, on whose efforts as well as their own everyone's hopes of a successful end to the war had to rest.

From these forces' point of view, intelligence about the enemy was of first-rate importance. All commanders depended, for every plan they made, on knowledge of who and where their enemy was and what he was doing. Much of this knowledge they could get for themselves, through active patrolling; some of it a very few of them could get from decipher; but much more information could be made available to them, if they could get in touch with eyewitnesses actually on the occupied spot.

Some units in the Allied armies, such as armoured car regiments, specialized in patrolling for intelligence – not all with the daring of Bob Melot of the SAS, who spent several days sitting beside the roadside in North Africa, wearing a sheet over his uniform, and noting particulars, which he wirelessed back to base each night, of the Afrika Korps as it drove past this apparent Bedu. Navies necessarily included patrol craft, not made much less useful by the introduction during the war of radar: sightings by eye were then almost always much more informative than sightings on a radar screen. Air reconnaissance and ground intelligence provided from resistance sources could be knitted together firmly to provide excellent information, on which tactics and even strategy could be based.

Almost any news from enemy-occupied territory was worth having. What came out officially by Axis broadcasts was certainly worth listening to, and equally certainly had been doctored by the Nazi propaganda machine before being put on the air. Broadcasts at least could be picked up immediately; newspapers, much fuller of nuggets for the intelligence analyst, might take weeks to get into his hands. It is true that there was a constant traffic of both sides' secret agents, in both directions, but this was not the sort of traffic that could easily manage armfuls of newspapers. Most newspapers from occupied Europe that reached London at all had to come round through Lisbon or Stockholm or Vladivostok, and on by sea or air. Moscow, not being at war with Bulgaria (except for a few days in September 1944), could do a little better, traffic across the Black Sea allowing. Washington, being farther away, necessarily did worse. Main news items could be picked up fast enough in Switzerland, and wirelessed out; the intelligence requirement was rather for such items as the stock exchange prices and the small advertisements.

Newspapers provided invaluable economic intelligence, in spite of all the efforts made by censorship to keep vitally important items from being published. A spy – *provided he or she could communicate* – was of course a far better source than a newspaper for this kind of information, but hardly any of the wartime spies of whom we know was rightly placed for this work, in a big government office. Significantly enough, the best-known case is that of Harry Dexter White, who worked in the United States treasury for the secret services of the USSR, which were supposed to be on the same side as the United States in the war, not against them. There may be other cases, that have never come to light: the truly successful spies are the ones whose names never get into the news media, at least in their lifetimes.

Less sensational, much more practical work could be done by people far from government directing staffs, who yet had economic data under their hands that mattered: railway clerks. Ideally, an intelligence network would include a clerk-typist at a main railway junction, who worked in an office so large that no one would notice if he (or she) took an extra copy of everything typed, and took it home in the evenings. This, like so many tricks of the intelligence trade, is an old one: the senior typewriter (in those days a person, not a machine) in Dublin Castle in 1919, a highly respected lady who had been many years in government service and did all the really secret typing, had an extra copy of everything she typed in Michael Collins's hands by seven o'clock every weekday evening. No wonder Collins saw the backs of the British. A Belgian intelligence circuit, run by a man who had done the same sort of thing in 1914–18, had a similar agent on the station staff at Namur in 1942–3, who saw and collected notes (among other things) on all the goods traffic between the Ruhr and the U-boat bases along the Biscay coast of France. This material he passed to his secret chief, who was able to transmit it to the Belgian government-in-exile in London, usually by clandestine short-wave wireless. Sometimes, if the sheer bulk was too great to be compressed into a telegram, the RAF would send a light aircraft across to fetch suitcases full of it.[7] Either way, the data soon got to the British admiralty and helped to decide the Battle of the Atlantic, one of the most crucial of the war. More on the methods of transmission – a vital point for clandestine workers of all kinds – when we come to actual examples later on.[8] We need to go into more detail about what got transmitted.

A great deal of economic intelligence was available in print, for those who had the learning and the energy to quarry it out of great libraries. Europe's geological resources, for example, were fairly accurately known before the war, so that the importance of (say) Albanian and Turkish chrome deposits to the German steel industry was a matter of common knowledge to the experts on both sides. The efficiency with which known deposits were worked was another matter, something that resistance sources – industrial spies, in fact – could well discover. Production figures, not only of course in mining, were of crucial importance; so were the state and the direction of trade. Railway sources were fairly readily available, in London at least, for all this, thanks to the strongly anti-Nazi attitude displayed by railwaymen over most of western Europe, and to some adroit organization.

Railway sources, of course, were indispensable for another crucial item, this time of strictly military intelligence – news of movements of troops and warlike stores. The best way for a general to guess what his opponent is next going to do, is for him to study what troop movements are going on; for millennia past, great commanders have needed first-rate intelligence to secure their victories, and regular news of movements is a prime source of first-rate intelligence. By studying movements in progress, plans can be inferred and counter-measures can be got ready.

Like most weapons in the intelligence world, this one is two-edged – sometimes you can feed false news of movements to your enemy, and so deceive him. Stalin got accurate reports of German troop and aircraft movements in the spring of 1941, from Comintern agents of his own, that pointed clearly to an impending German attack on the USSR. Richard Sorge, his spy in the German embassy in Tokyo, even gave him the exact date, though Sorge's message may not have been deciphered in time. But Stalin got similar information from the royal government of Yugoslavia in exile, and from Churchill, and from Roosevelt; so, thinking it was a capitalist plot to deceive him, he ignored all the reports – an expensive mistake.

Hitler made an expensive mistake as well, three years later. Unknown to him or to his staffs, the British had captured or converted – 'turned round' is the term of art – *all* his spies in this country, and they fed him for months with reports, which he believed, of a large American army in Kent and Essex under General Patton, threatening Calais, and an Anglo-Polish army in Scotland, threatening Norway. Against these phantom forces he kept over forty divisions deployed, while the Normandy landing succeeded; he had been deluded into thinking Normandy a feint.[9]

Next to movements, intelligence staffs need to know about locations – where headquarters are, which ships are in which ports (and at what quays, and in what state – there are no limits to an intelligence officer's curiosity), which aircraft are on which airfields, and above all exactly which army units and sub-units are where. This leads on to their main preoccupation – the enemy order of battle. That is, how are his forces organized, precisely? What is their command structure? What are the title, strength, composition and armament of every formation and unit? And in every case, what is the commander's name, how old is he, what is known about him?

A lot of this sort of information could be culled from resistance sources. From the earliest times, armed forces have gone in for fancy dress. The exigencies of modern warfare have compelled them, since 1914 at the latest, to give up the startling colours that graced earlier battlefields, except on formal occasions far from any front; but even khaki, horizon blue, field grey or olive drab left scope for badges, trimmings, flashes, and most units went in for them, in all fighting services. The German army distinguished the main arms of its service by different-coloured pipings on everybody's shoulder-straps, which anyone interested could learn, remember, and report. Individual formations in every army had their own particular corps or divisional or regimental signs – these, again, were memorable and reportable.

A vast amount of detail, in fact, about troop, ship and aircraft movements and locations became known to people in resistance; a lot of it was specially sought out by them, in response to inquiries from outside the occupied world. Inquiries and information could only pass to and fro through more or less elaborate networks, channels of communication arranged in deadly secrecy and at enormous risk, for the resister caught with material in transit would hardly ever be able to explain it away, and encountered not merely the certainty of a sentence, but the probability of a sentence of death – if anybody bothered to try him (or her), instead of mowing him down at once or packing him off straightway to the lingering death of a concentration camp.

Nevertheless an enormous amount of news about the German armed forces' deployment was available to their opponents, and until the early 1970s it was supposed that virtually all the behind-the-lines details of this news, that did not come from combat or from combing through printed sources, came from resistance. This, we now know, is not necessarily so. One of the best kept secrets of the war, which began as a kind of peacetime resistance operation and turned into a major staff triumph, was the success of Allied decipher.

The Germans had a ciphering system, based on the commercial Enigma machine, which they believed to be absolutely unbreakable. The Poles attacked the Germans' Enigma traffic when it began in 1926, and from 1932 to 1938 read a good deal of it. Improvements to the machine baffled them in 1938, but they kept at work, and gave mock-ups of it to the French and to the British secret services. When the Germans conquered Poland in 1939, all trace of this work against them was successfully hidden from them (apart from a hitch in 1943, not fatal), as were fifteen machines. The Germans remained in ignorance after conquering France as well in 1940, though a small Franco-Polish team continued at work in southern (then unoccupied) France. This team was whisked away to England when the Germans overran southern France in 1942, but was kept away from Bletchley Park in Buckinghamshire. There, a highly skilled team of cryptographers under Turing and Welchman the mathematicians and Alexander the chess master had since May 1940 been reading a great deal of the Germans' intimate conversations with each other.

Bletchley did not read everything – not everything could be intercepted, and a few codes (including the Gestapo's code) were never broken in wartime; but it read a great deal. Its findings were distributed, under the code word Ultra, to an extremely limited number of British and American senior commanders and staff officers. One of the Russians' best intelligence sources, Rudolf Roessler (Lucy), provided Stalin with such closely similar material that it seems possible that Roessler had some sort of secret link with Bletchley; though what that link was has never been established. Whether the Russians also broke and read Enigma traffic is not known either.

In any event, the highest Allied commanders – in the west at least – were quite often able to read Hitler's most secret and most immediate directives to his own principal commanders on various fronts. Moreover, as the Enigma machines were simple and were believed by their users to be quite secure, the Germans also used them – they had thousands of them scattered round Europe – for a mass of minor administrative detail, posting orders and so on, so that study of them produced a wealth of data about order of battle, as well as points of prime strategic and tactical import.[10] The Americans had a similar success with the Japanese diplomatic cipher, and though they bungled the warning it might have given them about Pearl Harbor, they were able to use it in the end to kill Admiral Yamamoto.[11]

Does this mean, then, that all the tremendous effort put into intelligence work by a myriad of devoted agents was a sort of colossal insurance policy, kept fully paid up in case the Germans ever tumbled to the fact that Enigma was not as entirely safe as they supposed it to be? Such a view would be exaggerated; but it must be admitted that, since the Ultra operation went public, the importance of intelligence networks in the general history of the war does not seem to be quite as cardinal as had earlier been thought. And though we have some studies on the general problem of intelligence, the published histories of the services that handled secret information in wartime are, Hinsley's series apart, nil. During the cold war neither the CIA on the American side, nor the KGB or the GRU on the Russian, cared to let anything be known that they could block; and since the end of the cold war they have none of them lowered their guard, though there are some fascinating defectors' stories.[12]

About escape a good deal more is known than about intelligence, through a series of escapers' accounts of what they have gone through, though there seems to be no published general theory of escape.[13] One or two points of outline may be made here; details will emerge in three of the chapters that follow.[14]

The Comintern ran its agents round Europe, indeed round the world, without much difficulty. It had an exceptionally efficient passport-forging branch, with substations in most European countries, and a communist of the eminence of Maurice Thorez could travel from Paris to Moscow with hardly more trouble than from Paris to Lille. No one should be so ingenuous as to think that such services were withdrawn when, for propaganda reasons, Stalin wound up the Comintern in 1943. However, virtually nothing about them has been published.

Less eminent, and less party-centred, people also needed to move about unobtrusively in Hitler's Europe, and a substantial proportion of resisters' effort went into helping them to do so. There were, for example, caïques plying the Aegean, in 1941–4, carrying to Turkey New Zealand, Australian and British troops left behind in the Greek campaign. The Danes were so efficient at hiding their Jews from the Nazis that only fifty of them were killed; over 6,000 of them were either hidden, or smuggled across the Sound into Sweden – a journey made by 11,000 other Danes as well. The Dutch hid over 30,000 Jews successfully; one whom they were not able to hide all through the war, Anne Frank, will long be remembered.[15] Her case has provided for countless teenagers their first introduction to anti-semitism. Over 100,000 Dutch Jews were rounded up, taken away, and murdered as she was: this was the sort of peril that escape workers wrestled against. A very few extra resourceful people could try to pick their way round occupied Europe by themselves; usually it was much more sensible to seek help.

As for subversion, it is important to remember at the start that there was hardly any trace of normal democratic life in Hitler's Europe. Only the Danes were allowed to have elections – once. The vote for Nazi candidates remained derisory, and the experiment was not repeated. Otherwise, Nazi control meant dictatorship, and not dictatorship of the Roman type either, when after six months the senate took power back from the dictator. The Nazis reckoned they knew what was best for everybody, and applied it.

Clandestine newspapers provided an obvious counter, simply to spread about the idea that, if one did not like Nazism, one might not be alone. Broadcasts from London, Lausanne and Moscow were of course highly effective in spreading news of how the war was going, if they could be heard. But in almost all occupied countries – following the example already set in Germany – it was a penal, occasionally a capital offence to listen to the BBC; and in some countries receiving sets were confiscated. The clandestine press was therefore important, though not as important as historians are going to try to make it out to have been. Historians like written evidence; lots of clandestine newspapers survive. Most clandestine editors, like most wartime saboteurs, are dead.

If one wanted to move beyond propaganda to action, sabotage was an obvious first step. A great deal of it is easy enough: if you work in a glass factory, take a hammer to work; in any factory, if the machine you use has a cast-iron base, hit the base hard with a sledge-hammer; if you are a filing clerk, muddle the files. More elaborate, sophisticated sabotage could be conducted by teams trained by experts; experts were provided by the Soviet secret police, then called the NKVD, during prolonged training in Siberia, and by the British Special Operations Executive (SOE). SOE's training schools in Hertfordshire and near Toronto produced thousands of trained saboteurs, including many members of the American Office of Strategic Services (OSS) who passed through the Canadian school. Plastic explosive was invented by one of SOE's immediate secret predecessors, and was available through SOE's channels to those working with it. This meant of course delivery, probably by parachute, in conditions of secrecy, and neither plastic, nor SOE's saboteurs, were available in large quantities all over Europe, simply because in places the range was too great. The USSR had a rule, hardly ever relaxed, which forbade aircraft working for anyone else's secret services to land on Soviet territory. So western Poland was at the limit of SOE's range, eastern Poland and the Ukraine lay beyond it.

There the NKVD was powerful enough to organize partisan bands in considerable strength, who wreaked a good deal of havoc on the Germans' communications. They worked under the close control of the operational staffs of the Red Army as well as the political police.[16] Farther west the NKVD had less control, and the locals had more say. In France and Italy sizeable armies collected in mountainous areas; in Yugoslavia three rival armies, one communist, one royalist, and one Croat separatist, fought each other as well as the Germans; in Greece also there were several rival bands, crystallizing eventually into a large one dominated by the communists and a smaller one kept in being by SOE. We shall not need to disentangle any of these Balkan complexities later in this book; even in France life could be complicated enough. A prefect of the collaborationist Vichy regime, who secretly sympathized with resistance, was held up five times in one day on the roads of his own department, the Corrèze, by five different armed bodies, each of which might have opened fire on any of the other four.[17]

A very few of resistance's sabotage acts were of decisive importance, particularly SOE's raids on the Norwegian heavy water plant in the mountains west of Oslo, which scuppered the Germans' plan to make an atomic bomb. And the cumulative effect of a very large number of very small attacks on their rear areas, both on the

15

eastern and on the southern and western fronts, was to depress the morale of the German army to so low a point that it was only able to fight with real efficiency in the closing months of the war, when it was forced back onto German soil.

There, there was no overt resistance – everybody was far too terrified of the secret police – except for a gallant but ineffectual students' rising at Munich in 1943 and the tragic failure of the generals' plot of 20 July 1944.

This attempt at murder by proxy, in the style now favoured with less elegance by the provisional IRA, shook Hitler severely but did not kill him, and provided him with an excuse to have done with the Prussian officer corps, from the heart of which it had been organized.

One of the continually moving features of resistance history is the way that the struggle so often bypassed the traditional governing classes, such as the officer corps or the civil service or the trade union bosses, and found its roots among ordinary people. Not many of the Roman Catholic hierarchy took an outstanding part in resistance; but outside Spain there was hardly a country priest in Europe who, when called on to help a resister to escape, refused to do so. Railway managers did what the occupying authority told them to do; railway workers set about disrouting goods and derailing trains. Shady men made fortunes on the black market; honest men formed reception committees to receive and hide parachute drops, once they had got that magical 'contact with London' or 'contact with Moscow' without which one could get nothing.

The following chapters will illustrate the sort of thing that resisters could attempt to do, through half a dozen particular examples. One will describe an intelligence network in France, 'Alliance', as it was seen by its founder's secretary, later Marie-Madeleine Fourcade. Two will deal with escape: Andrée de Jongh's 'Comet' line that conveyed aircrew in hundreds from Brussels to Spain, and Victor Gerson's more secret and longer-lasting 'Vic' network, which moved secret agents across the same countries. And three will bear on subversion. One deals with Jean Moulin, the one personality who might have replaced de Gaulle, but who came instead under his spell, united all the main strands of French resistance, and died under torture. Another handles Harry Peulevé, much more obscure but not much less efficient, an SOE agent who raised a private army in the Corrèze, was accidentally arrested, and escaped from Buchenwald. The last narrative chapter describes the work of Witold Pilecki, the man who let himself be sent to Auschwitz so that he could set up a resistance movement inside it, and then escaped to explain what was being done there. A concluding chapter will look at some of the problems these six cases raise for warfare and society.

2

Jean Moulin

Visitors to Chartres who can remember anything besides the cathedral may recall a huge brown granite fist clasping a broken sword: the city's monument to Jean Moulin who was prefect there when the Germans arrived in 1940.

Unlike the subjects of the later chapters in this book, Jean Moulin was a public personage, one in authority; someone who moved without effort or embarrassment among leading men, and was conscious of being one himself. During the war his task, of equal danger and difficulty, was carried through at the cost of his own life and in circumstances so heroic that he has become, next to General de Gaulle, the principal character in French resistance history. Every French schoolchild has heard of him; it is time he was better known elsewhere.

He was born on 20 June 1899 at Béziers, then a town of some 40,000 people, in a wine-growing area of Languedoc near the Mediterranean coast.[1] It had been much fought over since Roman times, and ever since the revolution had been well to the republican left. His father, who taught history in the secondary school there – and was therefore an anti-clerical republican – came from St Andiol, a Provençal village south-east of Avignon, and at Béziers and St Andiol Jean Moulin spent a joyful early childhood with an elder brother and sister. His brother's death from peritonitis when he was just on eight was the only serious cloud until seven years later the Great War broke out in 1914 and the world changed. It changed less in Béziers than in places where there was actual fighting, but all the

18

young men and men in early middle age went away to the front, whence far too many never returned.

Moulin missed front-line service. He was mobilized into the engineers in April 1918, at about the blackest moment of the war, but had only just finished his training, and had not yet been in action, when the armistice was signed on 11 November. Having steeled himself to face danger and death, he had a year of barrack squares and boredom instead, in a France where half the population seemed to be in mourning.

In November 1919 he was demobilized and went straight into the career on which he had set his heart: the public service. The prefect at Montpellier, where he had been a law student, took him directly into his *cabinet*, the group of private secretaries at his elbow who conducted the details of policy for every senior French official. In the twenty years of uneasy peace, Jean Moulin soared upwards in his chosen profession.

He had a quick, clear, divisive brain, having learned at his father's knee how to order his thoughts and keep them in order. He had sparkling eyes, a lively manner, broad shoulders, medium height,[2] grace of movement, and almost absurdly youthful appearance. Above all, he had charm: simply to be in his presence was a delight. He got through paperwork fast and neatly, and did not let his position as a public servant interfere with a subsidiary career as an artist and cartoonist. He collected pictures, as well as painting them, with a discriminating eye – Dufy, Rouault, Chirico, Marie Laurencin, Utrillo, long before they became household names. He was promoted under-prefect as early as 1925, at Albertville in Savoy, where, rather to his family's surprise, he met and married a very good-looking blonde called Marguerite Cerruti. The marriage was a mistake: she disliked life in the provinces, and quickly broke back to Paris. Within two years they were divorced. He never remarried, though he must have remained highly attractive to women; he devoted himself instead to his two careers.

One of his Savoyard skiing acquaintances, the radical pacifist Pierre Cot, became a close friend, and in December 1932 – when under-secretary for foreign affairs – called him to Paris. This brought him into the mainstream of world politics. From 1934 to the beginning of 1938, while Cot was Minister for Air, Moulin was his *chef de cabinet* and closest adviser – through the rise and fall of the French Popular Front and through the crucial first eighteen months of the Civil War in Spain.

Cot was not a popular figure among right-thinking people, either in France or outside it; Sir Alexander Cadogan for one, wartime permanent head of the British foreign office, could not stand him, and he has scored black marks from many historians. He was generally regarded at the time as a fellow-traveller of the Communists, if not an actual member of the French Communist Party; this may simply have been an example of the tendency, current then and since, to treat anybody of really radical mind as a damned red. Not until 1942 did the NKVD's office in the USA (to which Cot had fled in 1940) put up a proposal to make him a secret Soviet agent; it may be, of course, that the American office did not know that headquarters had already recruited him – but had they? The point remains open.[3] What is certain is that Moulin knew him well, liked him much, and worked with him. This in turn does not mean that Moulin was a Communist; his father had brought him up on the old republican motto, 'Have no enemies to your left'.

It was the Civil War in Spain that first introduced Moulin to clandestinity. Mussolini's Italy and Hitler's Germany were quite openly at work, aiding Franco's rebellion against the popular front government of republican Spain. Stalin's USSR was operating, hardly less openly, in the republic's support, although (a closely guarded secret) desperately weak from the great purge in the Soviet armed forces.[3] France was militarily weak as well, still exhausted from the blood bath of 1914–18, when 1½ million young Frenchmen had been killed to regain Alsace-Lorraine (population: 1½ million). The League of Nations was discredited from its recent failures in Manchuria and Ethiopia. The French government tagged along behind the British in the farce of 'non-intervention', a cover phrase for staying out of trouble. Good republicans were bound to be restive at the poor showing that the French republic was making in defence of the Spanish; was there anything that Moulin, as a public servant, could do?

Luck gave him an opening. Many devout French Catholics were as set on Franco's victory as devout republicans were set on his defeat, and Moulin happened to discover that a devout Catholic official in the Air Ministry was trying to smuggle a French air force aircraft to the Spanish rebels. As the price of his silence, Moulin browbeat him into smuggling a dozen aircraft to the Spanish republic instead. This was not an elegant proceeding, but it was efficient. Moulin felt he had struck a dozen small blows against the totalitarian menace he could see looming over France.

Though he could not see eye to eye with the appeasing government of the day, he was promoted in January 1939, on account of his undoubted abilities, to the post of prefect in an important department, the Eure-et-Loir – the great upland plain of the Beauce round Chartres, not far south-west of Paris. Here, the youngest prefect in France, he had a position of administrative power unlike anything found in England, below the permanent secretaryships of a few great ministries in Whitehall.

It was already plain, to anybody who cared to look, that another European war was imminent. Moulin felt that as he had just escaped the front-line risks of the previous one, he must make sure that he encountered them next time. Repeated requests to be called up with the rest of his class met with repeated refusals. When war broke out in September, and France's large army marched off to stay in the Maginot line while France's ally Poland was devastated in three weeks' *Blitzkrieg* and then partitioned between Germany and Russia, Moulin was stuck at Chartres, looking after call-up, blackout, food stocks, justice, road repairs. An Anglo-French force sailed to Norway; the Germans got there first and routed it.

Suddenly, the hammer of the *Wehrmacht*, the German armed forces, beat down the defences of the Low Countries and France. On 10 May the attack began; by the 15th the Netherlands had to surrender; Belgium gave in on the 28th. In the first days of June, ⅓ million men – two in every five of them French – were rescued from the beaches of Dunkirk, whither they had been rolled back behind a wave of German armour that had broken through to the English Channel. What Kaiser Wilhelm and General Ludendorff had failed to do in four years, Chancellor Hitler and General Guderian had managed in less than four weeks. After a short pause on the line of the Somme, the Germans moved on again; in a week they were on the Seine, on 14 June they entered Paris.

Ahead of them, away from them, westward, there spread a torrential stream of refugees: several million terrified civilians, mixed up with several hundred thousand disorganized troops. Much of this torrent passed across the Beauce and through Chartres, on its way towards the Loire valley, the west coast ports, anywhere quiet and remote, anywhere to hide. For four days, 11–14 June, Chartres seethed with people and vehicles, and then the flood passed on, carrying with it nearly all the car- and cart-owners of the places it passed through, leaving behind a trail of wounded, exhausted, dying and dead. Occasional German aircraft shot up roads teeming with refugees – partly to add to the confusion, partly for fun. Chartres was a road and rail centre important enough to attract a major air raid, which set a quarter of it on fire. By this time there were no firemen, no gas, no electricity, no telephones, no bread and very little water.

Jean Moulin stayed at his post, though he did not sit much at his desk. He saved the water supply, saw that the fires were put out, organized fuel for bakeries, made sure the wounded got nursed, had the dead buried. Even the Germans appreciated the amount of work he got through. Yet it was a rule of their occupation policy to leave no strong men undiscredited among local leaders. They picked at once, at hazard, on something to discredit him; this was behaviour they thought quite normal.

They found a pile of mutilated corpses, most of them women and children, and on 17 June required the prefect to sign a declaration that they had been mutilated by French West African soldiers. No evidence was produced. The corpses looked to Moulin like air raid victims; he refused to sign. For seven hours he was interrogated, browbeaten, beaten up; he still refused to sign. He was shut up for the night, first with a woman's corpse, then in a stone hut with barred windows from which the glass had been blown in. He felt he had made protest enough, lay down on a cast-off mattress on the filthy floor, picked up a sliver of broken glass, and cut his throat.

At five in the morning a sentry, glancing through the broken window, saw his body, weltering in blood; he was unconscious, but alive. In the French hospital he was recognized from his prefect's uniform, his throat was stitched up, and blood transfusions brought him round. Within twenty-four hours he insisted on returning to duty, remarking to the doctor 'I can still be of some use'. For the rest of his life a jagged great scar on his throat reminded him daily that he had been given back his life. To conceal the scar, he took to wearing habitually a cravat or a scarf. That he had his life to lose again made him not more cautious, but less. The accident that he had cut into a vital artery, but not through it, made him the more anxious to do everything exactly right next time.[4]

The Germans were impressed enough with his gesture to drop the affair of the mutilations altogether. They brought with them, automatically, complete control of the press (the underground press, outside their control, developed later), so there was no newspaper sensation, even locally, about the attempted suicide. It would in any case have been hardly more than a *fait divers*, a column-filling snippet, at the moment of France's catastrophe.

This is not the place to go into the military, or the political, or the administrative disaster which overtook France that summer; we are pursuing the fate and the courage of one man. By the end of July 1940 his department's roads were still littered with wreckage, but the crops were ripening as usual, and a few men were already trickling back from the army to help the women harvest. None of the French yet knew that the Germans proposed to take the bulk of the harvest for themselves. France had been cut into two halves by the armistice of 22 June; the Eure-et-Loir in the northern half was separated from the new capital, which settled at Vichy, by a new frontier – called the demarcation line – guarded by French and German police and only legally crossable with an *Ausweis*, a German pass. At Vichy, Marshal Pétain, the self-appointed Chief of the new French State that had replaced the Third Republic, governed by decree. Elections and parliamentary life had stopped.

In the autumn, a set of Vichy decrees instructed prefects on both sides of the line to dismiss left-wing mayors of towns and villages; not only communists, whose party had been illegal since October 1939, but all those returned by a popular front vote. This was more than Jean Moulin's republicanism could stand. He took no action, and in November 1940 was relieved of his post.[5] The Germans had been so impressed with his competence and fairness that they mounted a guard of honour to see him to the station, as well as giving him an *Ausweis* to go south.

He went back to St Andiol, and settled down, ostensibly like a good Voltairean to cultivate his garden. Like a great many other senior men out of a job, he rented a room on the south coast, and hunted up some old friends. His picture collection ensured that he was not short of money; it contained nothing so startlingly good that it roused the covetousness of Goering, who was busy fattening his own collection with canvases looted from the French, mainly from Jews.[6]

Moulin appeared to be an affable man in early middle age, in no way ostentatious, idling his time away in the pleasantest part of unoccupied France: as so often, appearance belied reality. He was in fact extremely busy, sounding out the possibilities of resistance, assessing the worth of leaders and of embryo movements, and debating with himself what part he could most usefully play.

As he gathered up the reins of political resistance, such as it was, in the southern zone of France, very few people had any idea that he was doing anything of the kind; those very few were, he knew, reliable. Before he embarked on any serious resistance work, he paused to think over how it should be done: a step few French people had bothered to take. Foolhardy resisters were quickly noticed, by policemen trained to look out for signs of foolhardiness. Jean Moulin was quite as brave as they, and a good deal more cautious; for the time being therefore, he avoided trouble with the police.

When he was dismissed he had thought of leaving France straight away, and inquired of a former subordinate about the chances of an exit visa. The man he asked, anxious to curry favour with the new regime, warned Vichy that Moulin contemplated going abroad, and all frontier posts were warned not to let him through. A better friend told him about the warning, so he set out to create himself a new identity.

First, essential stroke of luck: an officer he knew gave him a blank demobilization form. He filled this in in the name of Joseph Mercier, born at Péronne in 1896 (Péronne town hall had crumbled to ruin, with all its records, in the fighting of 1916), a law teacher in a middle western American university, who had lost all his papers at Dunkirk. From this starting-point he created a whole personality, secured a passport and got an entry visa to the USA as Mercier. Having been twice refused an exit visa by an official at Nice, he called at the office on a public holiday, walked past the dozing concierge, tried the drawer of the official's empty desk he thought most likely to contain the visa stamp, found it unlocked, stamped his own false passport, and then set about getting Spanish and Portuguese transit visas.

Iberian officials not being noticeably brisk, this took six months, from February to August 1941. During those six months Moulin travelled widely in south-eastern France, and once to Paris; usually as Mercier, usually staying in small hotels. Once at a restaurant a former close colleague in the Air Ministry came up to him with a cry, 'My dear Jean, what a delightful surprise to find you here!' He got the calm reply, 'My name, sir, is Joseph Mercier, I think you have mistaken me for somebody else.' Moulin trusted him all right, but knew his friend had made his peace with Vichy; he had taught himself the first golden rule of resistance, never take an avoidable risk.

This humourless and curmudgeonly behaviour was quite unlike his usual sparkling self; it was part of the personal burden everybody of weight in resistance had to bear. And how did Moulin come to carry weight in resistance? – by exercising his wit and his charm on those he met, so that they recognized his integrity and trusted him to help them. During the winter of 1940–41 it became clear that the war, which on most of the continent had been supposed all but over in July 1940, would last for some time. During the late summer of

1941, the Germans' failure to wipe the floor completely with the Russians, as they had done with the French, made a German victory seem less likely. Moulin went on quietly, gently, unobtrusively, irresistibly, encouraging people to resist, and finding out how resistance could and could not work.

By August he had discovered enough. He had detected four main groupings, and believed himself empowered by the leaders of three of them to get out to London, if he could, and report what was going on to General de Gaulle, whose rallying cry of 18 June 1940 had been heard directly by very few, but whose name and stance had become known through the BBC. These three groupings were called Liberté, Libération Nationale and Libération; the first two of them soon fused into a single organization called Combat, headed by the redoubtable Henri Frenay, and including on its propaganda staff the equally formidable young novelist Albert Camus, who ran the underground newspaper of the movement's name. Fourth there were the Communists, who had at last, after the German onslaught on the USSR on 22 June 1941, escaped from the ambiguous fix they had been in since 24 August 1939, when the Ribbentrop-Molotov pact had made them followers of the Germans' friends.

Frenay and his organization were frankly anti-Communist; they had in fact, precisely for that reason, received warm offers of support and money from American agents in Switzerland. Moulin, like Frenay, prepared to put his trust in de Gaulle, whom most senior Americans at that stage abominated, not liking generals in French politics. It was noticeable, as Moulin said in a report he put in on reaching London, that communist activity had sharply increased in July and August, for the obvious reason that, the more of it there was, the more German effort might be diverted from the attack on the USSR. Moreover, he added, if the non-Communist movements whose spokesman he claimed to be got no support – or too little support – from de Gaulle and from the British, the result would be to drive the thousands of French people who now wanted to join resistance into the Communists' arms.[7]

Long, long afterwards, Frenay alleged that Moulin had in fact been a crypto-Communist; in a cold war context, the allegation was often repeated. It seems to the last degree unlikely. He may have helped the Communists, by policies that he intended to help France, because after 22 June 1941 French Communists like Russian ones became ardent patriots. They worked with unusual ardour and devotion to get the Nazis out of France, and suffered such heavy casualties that they took the name of *le parti des fusillés*, the party of those who were shot. Not many fixed ideas are traceable behind Moulin's wartime actions, but his aim throughout seems to have been to restore republican order, not to overturn it; remember moreover his father's injunction to have no enemies to his left.

He got to London without mishap, under his false name of Mercier, by train to Lisbon (9–12 September 1941) and thence, after a six weeks' wait for a place by air, to Bournemouth. Happening to know neither de Gaulle nor any of his entourage personally, he had with typical thoroughness equipped himself with his own prefect's identity card, cut in two. One half he hid in his toothpaste. He borrowed a curved needle, thread and wax from the village cobbler at St Andiol, and sewed the other half inside his suitcase handle – so neatly, said a friend who saw it, that he might have been a saddler by trade.

In Lisbon, with the help of a hint dropped to the American consul in Marseilles while getting his visa, he met L.H. Mortimore, an anchor man for SOE in Iberia. Even Mortimore could not get him immediately onto an aircraft for London; there was a long queue, and a complicated system of priorities with which not even SOE could fiddle. In the month and a half that Moulin had to wait, Mortimore saw a good deal of him, and, years afterwards, wrote to his sister to say that of all the many resisters he had met, none had impressed him more deeply. 'His patriotism shone out of him, his personality compelled you to notice and to admire him.'[8]

SOE's headquarters in Baker Street, forewarned by Mortimore, looked forward eagerly to his arrival in London; so did de Gaulle's smaller but more elegant Free French establishment in Carlton Gardens. SOE already had four separate sections working into France – EU/P which dealt with the large Polish minority, DF which

27

ran escape lines, RF which worked hand-in-glove with the Gaullists, and F. F prided itself on its independence, and was therefore anathema to de Gaulle, who thought that nobody should operate into France without his own knowledge and consent. Its new head, Maurice Buckmaster, had a talk with Moulin, but was unable to persuade him to join F. Eric Picquet-Wicks, the young Inniskilling Fusilier captain who for the time being was in charge of RF, was always proud of having secured Moulin for RF instead, but the credit for that really belonged to a much higher authority, Charles de Gaulle.

Moulin was met on his arrival in London by André Dewavrin, known as Colonel Passy,[9] then de Gaulle's chief secret service officer, who took him to see the general next day. De Gaulle and Moulin took to each other instantly. Both were shy, proud, prudent men; each recognized traits of his own in the other; both were firmly devoted to the Republic. Each was the son of a professor (Moulin's father had received that title on becoming headmaster of his *lycée*), though the general, a regular officer by profession and a devout Catholic, was a good deal further to the right in his personal politics than the prefect, and had had a much stricter upbringing.

Moulin was the first man of any real consequence to come out of France since June 1940; had he wanted, he could have set himself up in opposition to de Gaulle, and tried to wrest control of the Free French movement from him. Instead, de Gaulle captivated him, as he captivated de Gaulle. As early as 4 November, the general signed a directive for him to take back to southern France, as the delegate there of the Gaullist committee of national liberation, and of the general himself.

To get there, Moulin would have to learn to parachute; the alternative route, in a felucca from Gibraltar with a rough Polish crew, was too uncertain and too slow. So he spent a few days at SOE's parachute school on the outskirts of Manchester, accompanied by Passy, who did a couple of jumps with him to keep his own hand in, and also formed a friendship with him. Several agonized weeks followed, waiting for a chance to drop. There were still only ten aircraft, eight of them already obsolescent, available in England for clandestine drops of all kinds; they then operated from Newmarket racecourse. Bad weather, and other exasperating hitches, prevented a take-off either in November or in December 1941; the Free French developed something of a persecution complex about this. It was in fact simply bad luck, but it meant that Moulin missed his chance of being received by friends in France.

Finally, after an appeal as high as the foreign secretary (Anthony Eden, later Lord Avon) had made sure an aircraft was available, Moulin was dropped, on the night of 1–2 January 1942. Communications with France were not flexible enough for him to be sent to a reception committee;[10] he asked instead to be dropped in the meadows near St Andiol, where he knew every hedge already. The pilot reported this had been done, but it is easy to mistake one moonlit meadow for another in open country, and he had in fact parachuted his party several miles off target, into a marsh east of Arles.

Moulin was separated not only from his home, but from his two companions, Montjaret, his Breton wireless operator and Fassin, his assistant, and Montjaret's transmitter, a heavy and delicate object, was not well enough packed to survive the drop. It was several days before all three met again, and several months before Moulin had direct wireless touch with London. Nevertheless he worked on undismayed.

For fourteen months on end he travelled clandestinely to and fro in France; never under his own name, never staying in his own house. (Besides the family house at St Andiol, he had a little place close by at Eygalières, a few steps from the orchard where Nostradamus had meditated on his prophecies some four hundred years before.)

The movements on whose behalf he had gone to London en- visaged propaganda as the main task of resistance, for a long time to come; at first he had been inclined to agree with them. He did a great deal for the underground press, including setting up a press agency under the young Georges Bidault. Bidault never forgot the care, the gentleness, the utter lucidity with which Moulin himself explained to him, in a quiet corner of a café beside the Rhône at Lyons, exactly how to construct a message in a code based on a fable by La Fontaine. But Moulin had a great deal else on his mind as well.

He foresaw that beyond the stage of propaganda would come, perhaps suddenly, the stage of action: it had arrived already in a few tempestuous areas, where hotheads had begun to kill stray Germans at random, sometimes at a terrible price in reprisals. Fifty hostages shot for every German officer killed was the habitual tariff: a heavy price for any country to pay or indeed to exact. In eastern Europe the Germans quite often exacted it, but in France they hesitated; to do so would run counter to the more or less 'correct' and respectful attitude they had so far taken to the French, whom they starved and pillaged, but gently: unlike the attitude they took to conquered Czechs or Serbs or Russians. The execution of forty-eight hostages at Nantes, in reprisal for a German officer's death, in the week that Moulin reached London did a lot to awaken the French to their duty to resist.

Moulin could see, ahead of most, that resistance was going to need arms before long; and one of his main achievements was to set up an organization to arrange for arms drops, and for landings and take-offs by light aircraft, all over the parts of unoccupied France that aircraft from England could reach. To this he added a parallel body to do the same in occupied France. This was work that had to be done in deadly secrecy by men and women he trusted, and who trusted each other; who hunted up suitably lonely fields, and set up parties near them who would, when the time came, receive and distribute arms and men. An immense amount of work had to go into this.[11] The end result justified Moulin's choices of men and methods, though he was not there to see.

Moreover, arms alone, even arms and instructors, were not going to be enough. The secret army that he was setting out to form had got to be articulated, had got to have some sort of staff, and some system of communicating with the Allied high command, with which it would need to work to send the Germans packing. Only a very small and simple staff would be needed, but something there would have to be.

Here he was less successful. His assistant Fassin produced a retired general, Delestraint, who had rank, record and standing enough for the job of field commander, and Delestraint was flown over secretly to London for an interview with de Gaulle, who had once served under him. The two generals got on well, and agreed to a reversal of roles. In October 1942 Delestraint was formally appointed chief of the secret army, under the cover name of Vidal, and was shortly flown back in again. Unhappily, he knew nothing of clandestine work and did not adapt himself to it easily.

Moulin meanwhile was as much on the move as ever. SOE's experts had taught him a little about disguises, and his habitual English-cut raincoat and scarf gave him a quite different profile from the one his acquaintances had known before the war. All the same, once when he was in Paris, his former wife, who had not lived with him for fifteen years, recognized him from the back – by his walk. She had the good sense to keep her mouth shut. A reliable Provençale friend, Madame Antoinette Sachs, used to follow a little way behind him when he was working in towns, carrying a wallet full of a complete set of papers to cover a different false identity for him. In case of need, he could thus become somebody entirely different in a matter of seconds, at the price of a prompt change of mental gear, to suit his new personality. He had also worked out for himself another golden rule of the secret life – never let *anyone* know where you are going to spend the night. He made innumerable appointments, but always for meetings out of doors, whence (if both were sure neither was under enemy watch) he and his companion could visit a café or a pre-arranged empty flat. He could get hold of people, they could not get hold of him. All this mass of detail he had to hold in his head; to write it down might be fatal. Moreover he had to hold in his head all the details of his various false identities, remembering from minute to minute not only who he was, but what his mother's maiden name had been and where he had been at school: such points as might get put to him suddenly at a snap control.

The details were bad enough, high policy was worse. He had above all to concern himself with politics, with the welding together of all the diverse strands of resistance into one single hawser, strong enough to strangle the occupier and the Vichy regime together.[12] In

31

October 1942, while Delestraint was away in London, he at last secured the agreement of all the main resistance movements in the unoccupied zone – the communists as well as the rest – to co-operation for the one military aim of evicting the Vichy regime with Allied help. Frenay only gave his consent on condition that he could be Delestraint's political adviser: a source of future friction.

This aim was something to which a great many of the French had been reluctant to commit themselves, hoping against hope that Marshal Pétain was playing some very deep game, was truly anti-German at heart, and at least was anti-communist. On 11 November 1942 those who had hoped great things of Vichy and the Vichy army were disillusioned. On that day the Germans, retaliating for the Anglo-American invasion of north Africa three days earlier, quietly overran the hitherto unoccupied zone of France. Resisters were taken utterly by surprise; so was the Vichy army. One, only one of its generals stirred; his troops did not follow him, and he was quietly arrested.[13]

Thenceforward everyone, in both zones of France, knew directly what occupation meant. And the military aim for the secret army became primarily to get rid of the Germans; secondarily, to overturn the Vichy regime. Moulin also founded – it is wonderful how he had the time as well as the energy to do so much – the *Conseil Général d'Etudes*, the general studies council (innocently neutral name). This consisted of a former deputy, two professors and a judge, with a third professor as secretary; it worked, till the liberation – first in Lyons; from April 1943 in Paris – on the juridical and constitutional problems of reconstructing the republic. In parallel with it was the almost untranslatable *Noyautage des Administrations Publiques*, a group of civil servants who looked into the problems of how to keep the state machine running during the change of regime for which they hoped, and of which senior civil servants had best be got out of the way. The more politically-minded chiefs of resistance, for whom suspicion was a professional necessity, were particularly suspicious of the CGE, regarding it as unrepresentative. It was indeed unelected, and had no one on it from the far left or the far right. Yet it was eminently just, well informed and secure and it did a great deal of preparatory work for the setting up of the Fourth Republic. The judge on it, Alexandre Parodi of the *Conseil d'Etat* became indeed Moulin's eventual successor as the Gaullist national delegate.

Moulin, having once set it up, let it be; he had plenty else to do, constantly weaving a sort of Penelope's web that was as constantly unpicked by accidents and arrests. He spent much of the worst of the winter of 1942–3 waiting about, in drenching rain, for aircraft or submarines to take him away. One aircraft was shot down on the way to fetch him, one submarine waited at the wrong beach, one extempore airfield had people on it talking German. At last, on 13 February 1943, he was withdrawn to England by Lysander for a short rest.

But he could not rest for long. He was too intricately involved with all the work of his delegation, he had no proper deputy, he could hardly bear to think about what might be going wrong while he was away. He and Delestraint both flew back, again by Lysander, on 21 March, landing not far from Macon, and having to undergo the scrutiny of a routine German railway station exit control an hour or two later. They just escaped a run of arrests that rounded up some three hundred of their colleagues, including Moulin's acting deputy Manhès, a very old and tried friend.

Moulin now had increased powers, increased range, and a still more important mission. All France now fell within his delegation's responsibility, and he had the task of creating a national resistance council, *Conseil National de la Résistance*, CNR, to oversee and direct resisters' work throughout the country.

Problems of allegiance in France were even more complicated than in most other occupied countries; only in Yugoslavia were there comparable strains on peoples' loyalties. In Norway and Holland the monarchs had gone into exile in England; loyalty to them was straightforward. The Polish and Czech republics in exile equally set up governments there. In Russia, it was hard to prefer the savagery of the Nazis to that of the nearby government of the USSR. In Greece and in Yugoslavia there were complications and in France there were grave perplexities. Pétain had abolished the Third Republic; de

33

Gaulle maintained it had never died, and impressed Moulin among many others with a strong sense of republican continuity on a somewhat mystical base. His was frankly a rival focus of loyalty, and in the spring of 1943 General Giraud was trying to set up a third, less ardently republican, focus in Algiers. Moreover the French Communist party, the one French party with some pre-training in clandestinity, having now escaped from its pro-Nazi phase, was ready to lead its working-class followers in whatever direction Moscow thought best. Moscow had little time to spare, just after Stalingrad, for thoughts about France, though Stalin did approve Eisenhower's deal with Darlan in Algiers, which shocked so many real resisters.

Some resisters held, passionately, that parties were abominable, the cause of all France's troubles; others held, with equal passion, that without parties the French could not express themselves politically. As one might expect, on a political matter the party-lovers had the best of it; the party-haters were elbowed out of the way by the party men, who re-established themselves as essential cogs in the machine of the resistance state that Moulin's delegation was trying to build. He had to admit parties into the CNR: would they all join?

It turned out that those which mattered any longer would, the Communists included. The Communists indeed, with typical dexterity, secured for themselves not one seat on the CNR, but two at least. Of seventeen members, Moulin alone was named, as chairman, in de Gaulle's order calling for the council to be set up.[14] Eight came from the principal resistance movements, including the Communist-dominated National Front, one from each of the two principal trade unions and six from political parties, including, again, the Communists.

At a preliminary meeting on 12 April, Moulin was assisted by Colonel Passy, who was on his first mission by parachute into France, accompanied by Yeo-Thomas of RF section[15] and by Pierre Brossolette, a strong and valiant Socialist who had been opposing the Nazis since before the war.[16] They made an odd trio; Passy a regular soldier, Brossolette a passionate democrat, Yeo-Thomas an adventurer who acted as bodyguard to them both. Brossolette and

Moulin fell out, for Moulin seemed to Brossolette too authoritarian in his manner, and too much inclined to arrogate power to himself. None of them had ever held any elected office; all were sincere democrats and republicans, but envisaged saving France in different ways.

Moulin, the incomers, Delestraint, and several military leaders nevertheless agreed on a system of coordination of armed action, Brossolette having done most of the preparatory work. The Communist Villon raised a difficulty: his party was, he claimed, already busy with direct action, and did not propose to ease up and wait for an impending Allied landing. Moulin, who had not been a civil servant for over twenty years for nothing, sought a formula of compromise, and dodged a direct confrontation.

Squabbles and personal difficulties continued to beset his work. Some leaders, such as Frenay and Villon, were frankly suspicious of the central power he wielded and, like Brossolette, thought him too authoritarian. Once – once – he lost control of himself, and fell into a shouting-match with Brossolette, each accusing the other of preparing for himself a position of power in the post-war France neither was to live to see. Otherwise, there is no clandestine meeting with Moulin on record from which whoever met him did not go away cheered and encouraged, with his faith in de Gaulle reinforced and his knowledge of ultimate victory confirmed.

On 27 May 1943, in a quiet dining room in central Paris, 48 rue du Four, the CNR held its first meeting.[17] Moulin presided. Everything went smoothly; the most important piece of business was the passing of a resolution supporting de Gaulle against Giraud, so strongly worded that its publication drove Giraud back into obscurity.

Soon thereafter, Moulin left Paris for Lyons, where – in spite of all its dangers – he felt more at ease than in the northern zone, where the Germans had been longer established and resisters' lives were correspondingly even more at risk. In fact Delestraint, who stayed in Paris, missed a clandestine rendezvous because he had forgotten the password, absent-mindedly signed his own real name when registering at an hotel, and was therefore arrested next day, 9 June. He died in Dachau.

Moulin was falsely reported to have attended the drop of an American OSS agent which had gone wrong – the Gestapo were waiting for him. This made a press sensation in the nineties, but was soon proved untrue. He was busy in and around Lyons.

Twelve days after Delestraint's arrest, on 21 June, Moulin was to take the chair at a southern zone meeting of military chiefs, in the house of Dr Dugoujon in the Lyons suburb of Caluire. Every possible clandestine precaution was taken except one – there was no way out of the house at the back. As the meeting was assembling, some black Citroens drew up outside, and German police tumbled out of them. Everyone in the house was arrested. One man, René Hardy the railway sabotage chief, broke away at once. (Hardy was tried after the war for having betrayed the meeting, and was acquitted. Someone, it transpired, had called out a rendezvous in the street, in the hearing of a senior Gestapo officer, who had followed it up. Some mysteries still remain, about Hardy's behaviour in particular; he had been in German hands a few days earlier, and – no wonder – had not cared to mention the fact to his colleagues. We cannot try to solve them here.)

None of the arrested resisters said anything at all for two days at least. This was a regular rule, to which everybody stuck who could; during the two days, one's unarrested friends were expected to move house, change identities, hide anything compromising. Brutal beatings gradually began to soften some of them up.

Moulin was beaten, all over, very severely indeed, for several days on end. Eventually he made signs – he had said nothing, and by now could no longer speak – that he wanted pencil and paper; they were brought. He drew a cruelly lifelike cartoon of Barbie, his principal torturer, and handed the pencil back.

They got his name, eventually, from someone else, wrote it down, and showed it to him – he could by now no longer hear, but could still just see: 'Jean Moulins'. He signed for the pencil again, and crossed out the final 's'.

It was his only admission. He who knew everything said nothing, and with heroic silence saved his friends.

One of his friends, held in the same prison in Lyons on suspicion

– his cover was that he was a barber – was sent for one evening to shave an unconscious, terribly battered prisoner, and found he was shaving the chief he knew as Max. Max came round for a moment, and murmured something in English, which his friend did not speak. This was Moulin's last contact with resistance.

He was driven to Paris and lodged in the villa of Boemelburg, one of the main SS commanders; visibly, he was dying. The SS were busy that week with a wave of arrests of Buckmaster's agents – some of whom were far too cooperative – and were anxious to get Moulin off their hands, besides being angry with Barbie for having ruined a promising interrogation.[18] They put him on a train to Germany.

It is not quite clear when or where he died – probably on the train, perhaps in or near Metz – probably on 9 July, possibly a day or two earlier or later, in Paris or in Frankfurt. Nobody wanted to undertake the responsibility of answering for him. Nor is it even quite certain that the ashes, presumed his, that are buried in his name in the Pantheon where France buries her great heroes, are authentic.

What is quite certain is that he earned his place there. It was he who united resistance, who concentrated the scattered energies of the French into the sole channel of anti-German activity, who saved France from the civil wars that ravaged Poland, Yugoslavia, Greece, who gave the battered nation back its self-respect. He never blew up a train, or knocked down a bridge, or even carried a pistol; he made sense of the work of those who did. As André Malraux said at the ceremony of the laying up of the ashes, in a splendid invocation to the dead and to the young, 'He made none of the regiments; but he made the army.'[19]

3

Marie-Madeleine Fourcade

Marie-Madeleine Bridou was born in Marseilles in 1909, into a family of the French officer class; not one rolling in money, but not a poor one. Her father, not himself an officer, was a leading executive in the great steamship line of the Messageries Maritimes, which handled most of the passenger traffic for France's then large colonial empire. She spent much of her childhood in the Far East, where most Europeans then led lives of pampered luxury compared with those of the peasants and workers who toiled round them; the sort of wholly comfortable, aloof existence that is today confined to the families of dukes and tycoons.

Readers who feel a shudder on discovering that they have to deal with someone born into the old colonial ruling class can recover at once; Marie-Madeleine herself was not in the least an oppressive type. Moreover she was brought up, necessarily for a member of that class in good faith and standing, in a set of traditions that can warm the heart, instead of chilling it; traditions that are now fading out of mind, to the world's loss. The French, like the British, officer class – if one can generalize at all about two bodies rather too shapeless to fit into any sharp sociologist's category – is centred on people imbued all through with the ideals of patriotism, service and honour.

Even the concept of personal honour is becoming rather hard to grasp, for people brought up in a world with such different fashions as our own. It had dominated the conduct of the best of the gentry of Europe for many centuries, and had often led to such absurd excesses as duelling, for which it is now chiefly remembered. Yet there was much more in it that was admirable than was absurd. Even after the desolation of the battlefields of 1914–18, that shook the faith of so many millions in progress and providence, there were thousands of families such as the Bridous who felt that serving one's own country as best one could was the highest task anyone could undertake.

In 1929 she married into another such family, called Méric. Her first husband was a serving regular officer. She bore him a son, a year after the wedding, and then a daughter, but the marriage foundered. They separated, she keeping the children; she had to find herself a job. This job, unexpectedly, provided training that turned out invaluable for her work in resistance.

She became the general secretary of a firm that published a group of magazines in Paris, some fashionable, some for entertainment, some political; she had a lot to do with one of the political ones, called *L'Ordre National*. As its title suggests, it was well to the conservative right in politics, though not with the conventional conservatism of the French bourgeoisie. The firm's and the magazine's organizer and mainspring was Georges Loustaunau-Lacau, a battlefield hero of the previous war, and a man of the utmost daring, capacity and rebelliousness. He was one of those people who positively relished being in hot water; wonderful to serve under, impossible to command.

He saw, far more clearly than most Frenchmen wanted to, two impending dangers for France: from Stalin's Russia and from Hitler's Germany. In the mid-1930s he organized a group of army officers, called the *Corvignolles*, to combat communist attempts to corrupt the loyalty of the armed forces. He saw, correctly, that France was at that moment rotten: he knew that his duty as an officer was nevertheless to save her. He had troubles with his supporters, and troubles with the police. Pacifically minded defence ministers like Cot seemed to him positively dangerous to France, and he resigned from the army in 1937.

Next he turned his attention to Germany, and set up a private intelligence organization to discover the real strength of the Nazis' armed forces. In the winter of 1938–9 he published his findings, including the outline German order of battle, in *L'Ordre National*.

This was the winter of euphoria, when people wrongly believed the Munich agreement had brought peace in their time. Hitler's swallowing up of Czechoslovakia disillusioned them next spring. Loustaunau-Lacau was so outspoken about the incompetence of the French high command, whom he did not hesitate to accuse of treason, that he was locked up in the first winter of the war. He was released on 10 May 1940, and went off quite without rancour to the front, where he was wounded and captured.

The wound was slow to heal, but he escaped quickly all the same. After the general débâcle, he collected a few friends round him at his place in the Pyrenees, at Oloron-Sainte-Marie; Marie-Madeleine among them. None of them accepted the fact of defeat; all were glad to follow his lead in resisting. They all moved to Vichy, to find out what was going on.

There they found every sort of disarray. The marshal who was supposed to be France's saviour was already eighty-four years old, and alternated lucid spells with an old man's futile reminiscence. He was surrounded by a mixed bag of patriots, politicians and men on the make, businessmen in search of a quick profit, intriguers who enjoyed hunting after power, still more petty intriguers out to ruin personal enemies; vain, corrupt, misguided men mixed up with sincere well-meaning men in a muddle, and a great many people who simply did not know what to do.

Loustaunau-Lacau had quite recently served on Pétain's personal staff, and was therefore able to get the great man's ear occasionally, though that ear was already getting very deaf. As cover for his real activity, he took up an obvious charitable cause – ex-servicemen's welfare – and had himself appointed manager of the *Légion des Combattants*. This put him in touch with everyone of military experience who was prepared to go on fighting, and innumerable excuses for travelling to and fro in France; the cover was so dense that one of de Gaulle's best biographers describes him as having 'sided with Vichy' at first.[1] To her equal surprise, alarm and delight, Marie-Madeleine was ordered from the start to handle the clandestine side of his activities. 'But Navarre' – already his codename – 'I'm only a woman!' 'That's another good reason! Who will ever suspect a woman?'[2]

Loustaunau-Lacau understood a lot about war, and could see from the start that news about the Germans' doings in France was going to be – was already – vital to those who alone at that moment had any chance of ever getting them out again: the British chiefs of staff. His *Corvignolles* provided him with wide-ranging acquaintances among intelligent people who trusted him, and who knew what points were likely to be of military value, and he was far too astute and far too mercurial a man to stick to one set of acquaintances only. Soon he had set up networks of observers in each of the main regions of France, who reported to Marie-Madeleine by messenger.

For years she had lived among regular serving officers, and understood their vocabulary; her work with *L'Ordre National* had familiarized her as well with the main ranks and formations of the German armed forces; she was, if anyone could equal him, as ardent a patriot as 'Navarre', and she had made herself a thoroughly competent staff officer. In a very few weeks, she found herself becoming a thoroughly competent spy as well.

She had every advantage of character and capacity for the task, except that she was the mother of young children, who could not always be parked with aunts or grandparents or friends, and that she happened to have inherited from her mother a slight but tiresome hip defect. This minor malady could sometimes become a major preoccupation, as disabling as a bad migraine, if she had to spend a long time standing or walking, and sometimes it gave her a pronounced limp. This was always a disadvantage in secret life, because it was something that caught policemen's and detectives' eyes, and once, late in the war, she had to miss a chance of making an escape because she was unable to run.[3]

At Easter 1941 she decided she had to take her son into her confidence, although he was only eleven. 'You do understand, don't you, darling? You're the son of an officer, the grandson of an officer, and must be sensible about all the family. If I don't write it's because I haven't the right to get caught; lots of people depend on me.' After

41

a few days' companionship, while she was busy receiving reports, arranging rendezvous, discussing technicalities, she added: 'I'm giving you a funny sort of holiday, darling.' 'Don't worry, mother, it's as funny as being at the circus, except that *we* seem to be the clowns!'[4]

Before long, she found herself in difficulties.

'Navarre' had got in touch with the British secret service, through one intermediary or another at Vichy; there was still a Canadian legation there, as well as a United States embassy, and for all his flamboyancy 'Navarre' had tact enough, when he had to use it, to manage the occasional discreet interview. He went to Lisbon – still using his *Légion des Combattants* cover – and met there by previous appointment, in a church, Lieutenant Commander Kenneth Cohen of the service's French section. The two men quickly appreciated each other's worth, and Cohen gave him a secret wireless transmitter and a book code. Loustaunau-Lacau got the transmitter out of Portugal simply: a Vichy diplomat sent it for him by diplomatic bag.

Once the transmitter was busy – there was no lack of former service signals staff to work it, and the book code was both easy to use and, in those days, hard to break – the network began to attract police attention both from the Vichy French police, jealous of any odd wireless goings-on in what a stickler for propriety could still regard as independent national territory, and from the German security authorities, who already regarded Vichy France as a satellite state. Marie-Madeleine, still in the initial stages of getting the network organized and finding out how to run it, was overwhelmed with messages and advice from two directions at once; from agents and would-be agents in France, counselling larger and larger risks, and from London, urging more and more caution.

Loustaunau-Lacau met a kindred spirit in Leon Faye, an air force major with no fewer than ten bars to his *Croix de Guerre*, who had been in the trenches in 1916 at the age of seventeen. The two of them went off to raise French North Africa for the allied cause, and were both arrested there in May 1941. Both at once escaped and returned to France, where they were promptly re-arrested. Marie-Madeleine simply took the circuit over, signing her reports to London with the code name, 'Poz 55', that fitted the eccentricities of the signalling system, and remembering to put them all in the masculine gender. It was some weeks before London realized that it was dealing with a woman.

She was brought out across the Pyrenees into Spain – an acutely uncomfortable nine hours doubled up under a pile of tyres in a diplomat's car – to get a full briefing from an officer of MI6, who was able to explain to her exactly what kinds of information the British armed forces, particularly the admiralty, sought. Some of her friends in the French Biscay ports were able to provide really first-class intelligence, invaluable in the Battle of the Atlantic; the battle that was so nearly fatal to British hopes of survival.

Her circuit, for example, spotted that the German warships, *Scharnhorst* and *Gneisenau*, were getting ready to leave Brest in January 1942, and reported accordingly. Unhappily for the Allied cause, the admiralty staff were deceived by false reports to the contrary, foisted on them by a hitherto excellent Polish circuit which had just been penetrated by the Paris Abwehr. The ships' escape up-channel on 11–12 February, under cover of luck, dirty weather, and a big radar jamming operation, was a naval defeat for the British, but improved Marie-Madeleine's standing with MI6, for it showed her information had been sound.

She worked with and on the advice of MI6 without any political doubts; she was not much interested in politics, and recent and current French history did not give her many grounds for being fond of politicians. 'Navarre' had been a friend of de Gaulle in the thirties, and tried to treat him as an equal; he was rebuffed. The London-based Gaullists had several large intelligence circuits of their own; the parallel existence of Marie-Madeleine's network neither helped nor hindered them. MI6 could do a little to ensure that these different groups did not overlap dangerously.

But MI6 was not infallible, in spite of its tremendous reputation, particularly in France. It had sent a wireless operator to Marie-Madeleine by parachute in August 1941; he is only known by his code name, 'Bla'. He made an odd impression from the moment of his arrival, dressed like a Frenchman in a London musical comedy, complete with striped trousers, bowler hat, and a little imperial beard; he never seemed to stop talking, he never bothered to lower his voice – which had a marked cockney accent – and he constantly asked questions. Far worse, he turned out to be a devout fascist, who had somehow managed to slip through the secret service's security checks. While appearing to work for the circuit, he was in fact looking out for opportunities to help the Germans, with whom his private sympathies lay. It took fifteen months, and several dangerous arrests, for his French colleagues to take in the full enormity of what he was doing. He was then informally tried, by a court of five officers, pleaded guilty to treason, and was disposed of.

This uncomfortable affair reached its climax – 'When troubles come, they come not single spies but in battalia' – at the moment of the Germans' occupation of Vichy France, on Armistice Day 1942 and within the same week as one of the circuit's most famous feats, the spiriting of General Giraud from the Riviera coast onto a British submarine. What intricacies of secret service politics in London led to this task of escape being entrusted to an intelligence circuit that was hideously endangered by it, we shall probably never know.

Giraud lived in a strategic dream world of his own, that had little bearing on the real war. When he got to Gibraltar, Eisenhower had to explain to him gently that Giraud had not been brought there to assume command of the 'Torch' invasion of French North Africa, which was already in progress. Marie-Madeleine described as 'a sort of strategic delirium' a long paper in which Giraud offered to stay in southern France and act thence as 'chief of European Resistance'.[5]

Comings and goings to get rid of 'Bla' and to put Giraud onto his submarine drew too much attention: the Vichy police, egged on by the Gestapo, arrested Marie-Madeleine. She happened to call herself Claire de Bacqueville (her grandmother's maiden name) at that moment, and had the odd experience of having to swap cousins' names with her plainclothes interrogator, who was a de Bacqueville in real life. Luckily, her elder sister's husband had persuaded the Vichy police to burn earlier files that might have compromised her; more luckily still, the Germans' arrival persuaded a lot of Vichy policemen to desert. She and Faye were both allowed to escape at once. Loustaunau-Lacau was far less fortunate: the Gestapo claimed him and he was sent to Mauthausen. Being tough, far beyond the common run, he returned, though with his wound of 1940 still unhealed.

There were to be too many arrests for comfort or peace of mind; whole sectors of the network were decimated or even put out of action, particularly in Normandy and round Paris where 'Bla' had done his worst. Faye went to England for a rest, and for talks with MI6; while he was there, he gave the network a name, the Alliance. Almost simultaneously, Marie-Madeleine in a moment of inspiration decided to name all her sources and helpers after birds, beasts, insects; when Faye came back, she told him he was *Aigle*, Eagle. For herself she chose *Hérisson*, Hedgehog – a choice that had a ludicrous sequel soon afterwards.

Early in 1943 she and Elephant, the retired policeman who was her head of security and kept the network supplied with false papers, were helping Magpie, her excellent British wireless operator, to raise England from a château in the Dordogne. She had a premonition of danger: imminent danger. Reception was excellent, Magpie wanted to go on after ten minutes. 'A kind of tremor possessed me. We must leave. Leave at once. "Elephant, switch off the power." Elephant switched off'; and they drove away. The dust had not quite settled in the drive when the Gestapo arrived, searching the château for 'Mrs Harrison'.[6]

As will be noticed, members of the circuit came habitually to address each other, to think of each other, by their codenames; and when the Gestapo discovered this, as they did before long, they named the circuit – Marie-Madeleine took the title for her war autobiography – 'Noah's Ark'. It grew eventually to a strength of some 3,000 souls: far too large for safety, but this was not the sort of crisis in which safety came first.

She did what she could to decentralize, spreading the load of work and responsibility onto regional chiefs, each with his or her own wireless operator working direct to England. Every main French port, and every large French town, was covered by 'Alliance' at one time or another, but perpetual attention from the Gestapo prevented continuous cover everywhere. However much she dinned into everybody the importance of security, people would tell their friends; word got round much too fast and too far.

She could never forget her children but she could now no longer meet them. Through a thickly lace-curtained window, she once caught sight of them on a Lyons pavement, 'thin and pale and looking utterly lost and helpless'. She decided to send them to a chalet that belonged to their grandmother in Switzerland. 'The escape route was blocked and the frontier bristled with incessant German patrols. Driven from pillar to post the children finally made their way across the frontier alone. At the last staging post the peasants to whom they had been entrusted had simply pointed out the direction in which the barbed wire ran, miles from their farm. My son, a future officer, came through the test with flying colours and saved his sister. He was twelve and she was ten.'[7]

Her Paris organizer, the Duc de Magenta (Saluki), grandson of the third republic's first president, also had to retire – on Eagle's order – to Switzerland; his duchess, called Firefly in the circuit, crawled through the barbed wire to join him, bringing their three small children with her, while pregnant with the fourth. At the far end of the politico-social scale, Marie-Madeleine had a lot of dealings with communists and with plain working men. She recruited village gendarmes as well as chief inspectors of police; soldiers and sailors as well as generals and senior naval officers, labourers as well as industrialists. One of her circuit's neatest escapes was made by a policeman turned concierge called Guillot, whose codename was Dromedary. He and his wife were sitting in the courtyard one fine evening slicing beans. A carload of German police drew up. 'Does Monsieur Dromedaire live here?' 'He's up on the fourth floor.' The Germans tore up the staircase; the Guillots quietly walked away, not forgetting to take their precious beans.[8]

Eventually Marie-Madeleine was persuaded by Elephant's arrest that there was treason in the network somewhere too close to herself for it to be safe for her to stay. On the night of 18–19 July 1943 she was brought to England by Lysander, with two friends, from a ground not far from Paris: apart from a brief uneasy wait in a ditch till nightfall, there were no troubles about this operation at all.[9] She spent the end of the night at a cottage near Chichester.

She was driven to London and put in a quiet, anonymous West End flat, where she was called on by a formidable figure in every way, (Sir) Claude Dansey.

An unfortunate junior staff officer in SOE once told me that in 1941 he heard that a course of action his section wanted to pursue was being blocked by Captain Dansey of MI6. Having just been promoted captain himself, he went round to 54 Broadway to have it out, equal to equal. Captain Claude Dansey, RN, made it plain to him that army captains were lower than the beasts that perish. Dansey was in fact pulling his leg; he was no more a captain, RN, than was the man he was talking to. But he held the equivalent rank of colonel in the army, and had the full personality to back it. And when the inquirer returned, discomfited, to SOE's main office at 64 Baker Street a summons from 'M' awaited him. 'M' – Brigadier, later Major-General, Sir Colin Gubbins, already the mainspring of SOE – gave him a further sharp reprimand for having wasted the time of the deputy chief of the secret service, and policy on the point at issue remained unaltered.

Dansey remained a power behind the scenes in Whitehall throughout the war, and was firm with Marie-Madeleine. He settled her in a house in Chelsea, at 10 Carlyle Square, where she could receive and comment on her circuit's messages, but for nearly a year he kept her from going back to France, in spite of her devoted pleadings. 'You've gone on long past the safety limits', he told her. 'According to the law of averages, an underground leader can't last more than six months. You've lasted over two and a half years. It's sheer witchcraft.'[10]

Eagle and Magpie came to join her in London in mid-August 1943. They returned to France by the September moon, and were arrested on arrival, one of the reception committee having changed sides. Eagle escaped, with two SOE agents, onto the roof of the Gestapo headquarters in Paris where he was being held – at 84 avenue Foch, near the Étoile – but they were recaptured by alert guards as they reached ground level. Eagle – Faye – had a ghastly winter, chained to an iron bed in a damp dungeon in the fortress-prison of Bruchsal near Karlsruhe; he was killed at Küstrin, north-east of Berlin. Magpie, 'appallingly thin and gaunt', returned just alive after fifteen months in handcuffs.[11]

Marie-Madeleine felt extra anguish when Magpie and Eagle went back, reinforced by another of her premonitions. When Magpie's set remained silent, she was almost overwhelmed. 'I had had practically no sleep for a week, and the reflection of my face in the bathroom mirror frightened me. My own eyes stared back at me like a fakir's. I said out loud: "I'm going mad. I have no right to go mad." '[12] And so she pulled herself together, and went doggedly on with her work; leading her circuit as best she could from exile, seeking revenge for her vanished friends, looking always for a chance to get back herself.

The Germans thought, wrongly, that their September wave of arrests had put paid to 'Alliance' for good. They underestimated the network's flexibility, range, and resourcefulness, and the fiery persistence of its absent commander. They also caught Eagle's successor on the spot, Swift – Paul Bernard the industrialist; by a freak of fate he survived. The Gestapo quite wrongly thought he was involved in the generals' plot to kill Hitler, that exploded on 20 July 1944, and held him for long months of futile questioning in the Moabit prison in Berlin, whence in the closing stages of the war he managed to escape.

Marie-Madeleine imposed complete decentralization on the circuit, and regional groups continued to provide first-class intelligence about the German war machine – ranging from an extremely detailed map of the defences round the Cotentin peninsula, on the eastern side of which the Americans landed on 6 June 1944, to significant details about the impending attacks on England by pilotless rocket bombs (V-1s, called doodle-bugs by their intended victims). She heard some of the first of these as they fell on London; the success of the Anglo-American landings in western Normandy gave her an opportunity to return.

Her hip of course prevented her from parachuting. She was put into France by Hudson light bomber early in the July moon, south-

4. Andrée de Jongh in 1941.

5. Witold Pilecki. This photograph
   was taken by the political
   department in Auschwitz.

4. Harry Peulevé during
   the war.

5. Victor Gerson about 1942.

1. Jean Moulin in clandestinity.

2. Marie-Madeleine in metamorphosis:

left: before the war.

centre left: as a housewife; prepared in
London.

centre right: from the Gestapo's search list.

bottom: on a false identity card for use in
Eastern France, 1944.

east of Paris, indeed within fifty miles of its centre. Obsessed by Eagle's catastrophe, she insisted on separating at once from the reception committee, and set off to hitch-hike towards Aix-en-Provence, accompanied only by Flying Fish – Raymond Pezet, a fighter pilot. Her cover story was that she was married to him; the real Madame Pezet was in safety.

Such was the state of confusion to which resistance and air action had already reduced eastern France that it took them several days to get to Provence. She quickly met Grand Duke, her regional organizer, the Comte des Isnards, whose most successful work had been delighting everyone except the Germans. Unluckily for her, the Germans were beginning to close in even on him, and tailed him to a block of flats which he had just visited for a short discussion with her. They arrived as she was coding for London some information he had given her a few moments before about the plot against Hitler. She popped the coding grid and the half-completed message under the divan, and sustained thirty or forty minutes' conversation – as Madame Pezet, a lonely refugee from Marseilles – about the horrors of bombing and terrorism. No, no one in the least answering to Grand Duke's description had called on her; no one had called on her at all. Just as the Germans were leaving, one of them glanced – a routine police gesture – under the divan and pulled out what lay there.

The Germans went berserk, and started to break up the flat. A furious corporal kicked at a hassock, which burst open, revealing a shower of 'Alliance' reports. Here was evidence enough and to spare. They hauled Marie-Madeleine away, not gently, and assured her she would be interrogated by an important Gestapo functionary at nine o'clock next morning.

What concerned her most was that Grand Duke was to call on her at eight, with a car, to take all the reports away: she had to escape overnight, or he would be lost as well. She was locked up for the night in the detention cell of the nearest barracks. The window was barred, of course, but was it not just possible that she might squeeze between the bars? Between one pair of bars there conceivably might be room. She took off all her clothes; perspiring profusely, with summer heat and with fear, she found her skin slippery enough to let her through, heavily grazed but still able to walk; she remembered to take her batik dress with her. It was past three in the morning, the sentries were in a doze; she was free.

She got to Grand Duke's farm in time to warn him. A few days later, the Franco-American landing on the Provençal coast drove the Germans fast out of southern France, just as the break-out from Normandy drove them out of northern France at the same time.

Marie-Madeleine moved on, with a few of her most ardent followers, providing tactical intelligence for the moving battle line in the east, till Patton's army ran out of gasoline, and the allied advance ground to a halt. She escaped, with some trouble, arrest by over-blown resisters, village tyrants with free French arm-bands who had been fighting the Germans for fewer months than she had years. She spent the winter in Paris, able at last to be more of a mother to her children.

In the late spring of 1945, when Hitler's Reich at last foundered, she went through its ruins in search of the arrested members of her network. Four hundred and thirty-eight of them had been executed, including a group of fifty-nine – old men, priests, a dozen women among them – whom an SS Obersturmführer called Gehrum had had shot, neatly, in the back of the neck, a few days before the end. He had an Iron Cross, first class. They had a single large bomb crater for a grave.

After the war she remained a devoted supporter of de Gaulle – under whom she had not worked while the fighting was going on – and did her redoubtable best for the interests of ex-resisters under the Fourth and Fifth Republics. Her private life improved with another marriage – she left five children when she died in 1989 – and she has left in her book a fine and lasting memorial to her circuit.

4

Harry Peulevé

Peulevé is a French name; the family's roots lie in Normandy. Auguste Léonard Peulevé, Harry's grandfather, ran away from home at fifteen, and for a time lived very rough indeed in Paris, among the *apaches*, selling rats for a living, during the siege winter of 1870–71, when rat became something of a delicacy in that starving city. The Commune's excesses were more than even he could stomach. He got himself a technical education, learned English, and became an engineer in Birmingham, developing several inventions in ammunition-making machinery that were highly useful during the Great War of 1914–18. He became a British subject, married an English country girl, and retired, a pillar of local society and something of a terror to his family – three boys and a girl – to a house near Stratford-upon-Avon.

His second son, Leonard Otho, married Eva Dallison, an East Anglian clergyman's daughter of much more powerful character than himself, a rival even to his own father in strength of mind. He seems to have been amiable rather than forceful, and to have had trouble holding down any particular job. He was the Paris agent of Carter's, the Surrey firm of seedsmen, when the Great War began. Indeed, his daughter Annette was born on 3 August 1914, the day Germany declared war on France and the day before Great Britain declared war on Germany.

Leonard Peulevé at once volunteered to fight, and became an officer in the Army Service Corps. Eva took the baby over to his father's in England but as soon as the western front had stabilized, moved back to France with her to be near her husband. Her only other child, Henri Leonard Thomas, was born at Worthing on the west Sussex coast on 17 January 1916. (His workmates and grown-up friends used to call him Harry, but to his parents and sister he was always Henri.)

Henri spent his childhood in almost perpetual motion. He was hardly weaned before his mother took him and Annette back to France, where occasional shifts in his father's location kept them from settling anywhere. At the end of the war, Carter's did not call their Paris agency back into being, and Leonard joined hundreds of thousands of other demobilized officers in hunting for an officer-type job. He found one in Algeria, where for a little while he was a British vice-consul, successively at Bougie and at Oran in 1920–21;[1] Henri got his first schooling in a nuns' kindergarten in Algiers. Thence they moved to England, and he had a spell at Rye grammar school. He was also at Shakespeare's old school at Stratford, while his mother was headmistress of a nearby village school. (Warwickshire, never the liveliest of counties, was then one of the few so poor that it would employ women teachers.) He also went to a number of private tutors, English and French, and spent a good deal of time with an uncle on the Riviera.

This upbringing might keep any child from getting bored; it was also thoroughly Anglo-French. From earliest childhood, he spoke both French and English equally well. In England he was obviously English. In France he could pass without any trace of effort as a Frenchman; in fact he was a Frenchman, in feeling, just as much as he was an Englishman, both in feeling and by birth. This duality of outlook and sympathy combined well with the forcefulness he had inherited from his father's father and his mother, and the gentle manners he had learned from his father, and with the liveliness of mind and strong inquiring turn he developed during his kaleido-scopic schooldays.

Frequent changes of school may benefit the character, but do not do much for the intellect. Henri did not try to get to a university, like his mother's father. Instead he followed his father's father's example and went to a polytechnic, at Earl's Court in London, where he qualified as an electrical engineer, with special interest in wireless (as radio was then called). On the strength of this, he was taken on by the BBC, and was a working cameraman on its early television team at Alexandra Palace. He worked three very long days a week, as a rule, with a whole day's rest between each, and supported himself easily enough on his pay.

His early twenties were troubled – as is common enough – by an unsuccessful love affair, with a girl whose mother laid down that a television cameraman was not good enough for her daughter. (The daughter married a Barnardo's boy in the end.) When the girl broke it to him that they must part, he had what would now be called a nervous breakdown; for a few days he lost his memory so completely that he recognized neither his parents nor Annette, did not know where he lived, and only seemed to remember in which pocket he kept his cigarettes. This state vanished as abruptly as it had arrived, and the family took care to tell nobody: his employers, then and thereafter, never knew.

Soon he was back at work, providing entertainment for the seven-thousand-odd television viewers of England on the eve of war. When war broke out, Alexandra Palace closed down, and he at once joined the army. His technical qualifications put him into the ordnance corps, with which he served as a staff sergeant in a quiet base depot, in the British expeditionary force in France the following winter.

The débâcle of May–June 1940 swept him away with the rest. He got out of France without any danger or serious difficulty, but the horrifying experience of having been in the rout was one that haunted him for years, until still more horrifying experiences came to crowd it out of his nightmares. There was little he had been trained to do, at that time, towards protecting his beloved France, but to see France so overthrown, without striking one actual blow for her, was almost more than he could bear. When he got to Liverpool from a Biscay port, he had to listen to the angry comments of old men, who remarked that they had not run away in the war before; they made him no more comfortable.[2]

The army needed him, and there was plenty of work for him to do. He was transferred, on being commissioned, into the newly formed Royal Electrical and Mechanical Engineers. He already knew so much about his work that he was promoted captain, and again found himself at a leading point in current technology. His task was to maintain and assess the performance of the earliest army radar sets, which were supposed to enable heavy anti-aircraft guns to hit their targets at night or through cloud. The degree of success was small, and the whole subject was wrapped in particularly deadly secrecy: it provided him with an early opportunity for learning to keep his mouth shut.

He was stationed at Uxbridge, on the western outskirts of London, at the headquarters of 1 Anti-Aircraft Corps. (I met him there once, quite by accident; shook his hand in the bar during a staff visit; was greatly taken by him, but never met him again.) There he could have remained, quietly *embusqué*, all through the rest of the war. That was not his idea of how he should spend his fighting time. He bombarded the war office, through any private channel he could find as well as through the correct ones laid down, for some opportunity to make use of his French. One or other of these moves, he never knew which, brought him an interview with Selwyn Jepson, who at once realized he had before him a recruit of unusual quality.

Jepson was the recruiting officer for SOE's F section, the non-Gaullist country section working into France.[3] From his profession of novelist he had acquired a good deal of insight into character, and he picked a number of astoundingly able men and women for this esoteric task, Peulevé by no means the least of them. He gave all the candidates he saw a preliminary interview of an hour or so, in a bare room in the requisitioned Northumberland Hotel off Whitehall, or in the war office building itself. He took care to emphasize the dangers, the difficulties, the loneliness of the task they might be going to volunteer to undertake. Yet in almost every case he found that he had made up his mind within the first minute or two whether each particular one would do; just as many of the people he met knew, before ever he met them, whether they would accept secret work in enemy territory if the chance were offered.

A war cabinet decision of July 1940 had laid down, when forming SOE, that it could demand the release of officers from any other fighting service;[4] so there was no difficulty about securing Peulevé's release from Anti-Aircraft Command. He went on the usual F section training routine: a few weeks at Wanborough below the Hog's Back for a preliminary course under a Guards major; a stiff month's para-military training on the wild west coast of Inverness-shire; a few days' parachute training at Ringway and a physically milder, but emotionally still more exacting, month near Beaulieu in the New Forest, learning how to be a secret agent.[5] On top of all this, his pre-war work picked him out for training as a wireless operator, so he attended SOE's wireless school at Thame Park. He could daydream through the lectures on theory, which he could have delivered himself, and the short-wave transceiver he had to master – morse transmitter and receiver in one small suitcase – presented no technical problems to him.

He emerged exceptionally well qualified for the task that lay ahead and in that closed world he made several friends. He particularly took to Violette Szabo, the widow of a French foreign legion sergeant of Hungarian origin who was killed in Koenig's Free French brigade at the second battle of El Alamein. She was a cheerful cockney girl, high-spirited and an excellent shot; her high spirits and Harry's probing, engaging manner and equally high spirits blended well together.

SOE had plenty of people, like these two, with personalities like sledge-hammers; people who made an immediate forceful impact on their companions, unless they remembered the lessons dinned into them in the New Forest about the importance for a secret agent of being inconspicuous. Some of them, however hard they tried to hide the light of their daring under a bushel of anonymity, could never manage to dim it altogether.

One of these extra forceful men, the thirty-five-year-old Mauritian Claude de Baissac, was being groomed in the summer of 1942 for a particularly important mission. He too took to Harry Peulevé, and chose him as his wireless operator and colleague. They were to go, via Provence, to Bordeaux, to see what they could do to upset that port's working. It was known from 'Alliance' and other intelligence sources that Bordeaux was still active, and in the summer of 1942 it had a special importance: it was the most accessible large port in German hands for blockade-runners from Japan. Several of these ships were known to be at sea, bearing cargoes of Malayan tin and rubber that German war industry needed desperately. Here was a worthwhile target; the stocky, fiery-tempered, uninhibited de Baissac and the equally uninhibited, imperturbable Peulevé seemed an ideal pair to tackle it.

F section provided them with a mass of contact addresses in Provence and on the Riviera, all carefully memorized. Their hopes were high, but ill-founded. The initial contact arrangement, for a reception committee to greet them on arrival, broke down at the Provençal end. They were in a hurry to leave, and determined to drop blind, in open and deserted country, and took off, in a four-engined Halifax bomber, from Tempsford near Cambridge on the night of 30–31 July 1942. They had an uneventful flight to the neighbourhood of Nîmes, where the pilot had no trouble in picking out by moonlight a large flat field.

By an unhappy error, he dropped them from so low that their parachutes barely had time to open before they found themselves on the ground. De Baissac sprained his ankle badly. Peulevé was much worse off: he broke his leg in several places, and could not even hobble. By two strokes of luck, de Baissac happened to stumble straightway on a helpful farmer's family, who carried Peulevé to shelter for the rest of the night, and then, better still, to find a local doctor who knew of a discreet hospital ward in Nîmes, to which the wounded man was secretly conveyed.

The fracture was so severe that a surgeon, who took care to ask no questions, had to be called in to set it. This was a major operation, and a discreet anaesthetist was available, but Peulevé insisted on being operated on without any anaesthetic. This now looks like quixotry or masochism; in fact it was stoic common sense. A man who is sober and conscious knows what he is saying; a man under anaesthetic might say anything,[6] and the agent felt insecure enough already without running any unnecessary risks.

After a few days, Peulevé was well enough to move about on crutches, and made for the Riviera to convalesce. De Baissac had work to get on with; he had already said goodbye, and gone to look for a way across the demarcation line and a start on his targets at Bordeaux, leaving himself for the time being with no wireless operator.[7] He had two great blessings to count – he was still alive, and he was not under arrest.

Peulevé, hiding in a villa above Cannes, was in some ways more fortunate still. He knew well the part of France in which he was lying low. This cut both ways, of course: he ran some risks of bumping into old acquaintances if he went out a lot. The state of his leg prevented that, and he was living with a family of absolutely devoted resisters. The son was already deep in resistance activity – an extra dangerous business at that place and time, for the Riviera crawled already with police informers, and there were too many self-promoting local leaders with no proper ideas about security or discretion. The daughter thought she could serve resistance best by looking after this handsome invalid, for whom she fell, heavily. This presented Harry Peulevé with a further series of agonizing choices.

Yet from the usual day-to-day troubles of a secret wireless operator he was free. His set, in its kapok and timber package, had failed to survive the low drop – it was quite unusable, unrepairable even, and he had its wreck safely buried. So he did not have to undergo perpetual worries about where his set was, and whether it was securely hidden, nor have to live in constant awareness of the exact time of day or night, with his whole life organized round his pre-arranged times for sending and receiving traffic. Nor did he have to face that great operators' bugbear, fear of detection by hostile police listening sets.

On the other hand, he had not gone to France for a summer holiday, and till his leg had healed there was nothing active he could usefully do. He guessed, correctly, that de Baissac would get word of their troubles through to England, and that SOE would parachute in another operator for the Bordeaux circuit; Roger Landes in fact arrived by the October moon. Peulevé was in touch with Peter Churchill, SOE's current man on the Riviera; he made exactly the same judgement of Churchill's local contacts as de Baissac had done a few weeks previously. That is to say, he thoroughly distrusted them

– they seemed to him to be either frivolous, or downright dangerous. So dangerous indeed did the whole neighbourhood seem to him to be that, as soon as he had acquired fair skill in moving about on crutches, he left.

He left in the company of the young Jacques Poirier, who had been looking for years for something active he could do, and wanted to get out to London to join the Free French forces.[8] The devoted daughter of the Villa des Ames Perdues, as the last thing she could do for Harry, queued for hours to get him a ticket and a seat on the train to Perpignan (SOE's money covered this). From Perpignan, he and Poirier set off into the Pyrenees.

They thought they had secured a reliable smuggler to guide them. He simply abandoned them after he had been paid. By sheer luck, they ran into him again and behaved in so threatening a way that he took them as far as the frontier after all, without being paid a second time. Peulevé was still walking with difficulty – Jepson, writing on him in the *Dictionary of National Biography*, maintained he was still on crutches.[9] They used mountain paths near the Mediterranean coast that were not unthinkably steep, and took more time than was usual over the journey. But once they crossed into Spain, they promptly fell into the hands of the Spanish police, and spent uncomfortable months in prison at Figueras – twenty in an eight-man cell – being strip-searched and shaven on arrival, and bullied and underfed thereafter.

Poirier managed to smuggle out a letter to the British embassy in Madrid, from which an attaché came to rescue them – for each claimed officer status, Peulevé in the Royal Canadian Air Force and Poirier in the Canadian army (both quite untrue). The attaché managed to get them transferred to an hotel at Jaraba, where they remained under house arrest; at least they missed Miranda.

Miranda was a dump: a vast dingy hutted camp near the upper Ebro, not far from Franco's civil war capital of Burgos, in which flotsam and jetsam from that war and the world war rotted away. 'Parthians, and Medes, and Elamites', Balts, Lascars, Malagasys, Venezuelans, Malays; holders of Nansen passports, unsettled for twenty years; holders of none, unsettled for good; Belgians, Czechs,

Poles, Frenchmen, a human chaos. Many SOE agents were long pinned there: a stay of several months in this or another camp was a probable hazard of any wartime Pyrenean crossing. A fellow F agent of Peulevé's, whom he met at Jaraba, put it that 'After the squalor of Miranda, Jaraba was paradise'.[10]

Peulevé concentrated on leaving his leg to heal up, on perfecting his Spanish, of which he had picked up a smattering from servants as a child in Algeria, and on keeping out of everybody's way. For this last task he had an unusual gift. At two inches under six feet, he was a shade above average height; his grey-green eyes were large, and could be piercing; yet he was able to hood his personality from a casual gaze. He could turn himself off, much as he could turn off a switch or a tap, and sit quietly against a wall, wholly unnoticeable. When he was hiding from hostile police, this sort of portable personal camouflage was a considerable help.

He still had money with him and on 11 April 1943 got away from Jaraba by a simple escape. He damaged his teeth enough to need to visit a dentist in the town and then, instead of returning to his hotel, hailed a taxi and was driven to Madrid. He was welcomed at the British consulate, arranged for Poirier's release, and within a month was back in London. He marched into the office of his head of section – or rather, into the room he used in a flat where the section met agents, on the eastern side of Portman Square, saluted smartly and said 'Sorry I made a balls of it, sir. When can I go back?'

Maurice Buckmaster, to whom he spoke, was delighted to see him again. F section, never short of heroes or heroines, was always short of wireless operators, and to have a wireless operator available who had already proved himself as brave and as resourceful as Harry Peulevé had done was a rare advantage. He had a few weeks' leave, during which he renewed his friendship with Violette Szabo and was discreetly shown off, under the name of Captain Poole, to agents under training. He could, once more, have been quietly *embusqué*, had he wanted, in SOE's training section; instead, he kept pressing to be sent on another operation into France.

He went back to Beaulieu for a short refresher course, to remind him of a secret agent's responsibilities; he hardly needed reminding about the essential feature of clandestine life, for he had soaked up that lesson already in a harder school. It was, as T.E. Lawrence had put it a generation earlier for his British companions in the Arab war of liberation against the Turks, to do one's best to get accepted entirely, as a companion and not as a stranger. 'Keep always on your guard, never say an unnecessary thing. Watch yourself, and your companions all the time. Hear all that passes, search out what is going on beneath the surface.'[11] It was a task that called for perpetual personal tension; Peulevé longed to get on with it.

His chance came quickly. To understand how it arose, and into what dangers it promptly led him, a few words are needed on the work of some other F agents in France.

The whole shape of occupation had altered while he was in Spain, for in November 1942 the Germans had overrun the hitherto unoccupied two-fifths of France that Pétain governed from Vichy. Vichy's voice in French affairs became more feeble than ever. De Baissac, among several other F organizers, had secured more promises of work against its regime, now that only the shadow of independence was left to it. His main work still lay around Bordeaux, in the zone the Germans had been occupying since June 1940, and he often visited Paris by train as well. In Paris he had accumulated a personal following, under a Frenchman with an Irish surname – Marc O'Neil – who was descended from one of the Irish soldiers who had gone into exile with James II (de Gaulle himself was descended from another). He only narrowly escaped from the disasters that overwhelmed many F section agents in Paris in late June and early July 1943; disasters that stemmed partly from sound police work by the Gestapo, partly from the agents' own imprudence – they were too fond of each others' company – and partly from ineptitude in London, by inexperienced staff in F section particularly.

De Baissac handed O'Neil's group back to his second-in-command, a Frenchman of his own age whom he had left in charge at Bordeaux, and came back to England with his sister Lise, a steady companion in his work,[12] by one of SOE's private airlines on 15–16

August. They shared their Lysander with Buckmaster's assistant, Nick Bodington, who had just spent a month reconnoitring the damage in Paris. Bodington's stay had been arranged by the Frenchman who ran the airline, Henri Déricourt (codenamed Gilbert), and Bodington thought his own freedom from arrest proved Déricourt's soundness.

Looking back, we can now see he was wrong. Déricourt was in fact working hand in glove with the Germans, and had even dared to hint something of this to Bodington (they had been fairly close friends since before the war, when Bodington had been a journalist and Déricourt a civil pilot in Paris).[13] The feeling that, because you know somebody, he or she must be reliable is a thoroughly human one, but in the secret service world, also thoroughly dangerous.

What Déricourt did – how willingly is not a question we need to answer here – was to let the German security authorities in Paris, the *Sicherheitsdienst* of the SS, know in advance when and where he was arranging supposedly secret landings for light RAF aircraft. He also let them photocopy agents' letters from France to England that passed through his hands. This was a great help to the Germans, and enabled them to unravel several important groups of agents, including several of de Baissac's friends. They sent observers down to the country to watch from behind hedges the landings that Déricourt supervised, and tried to notice who left for England, and to follow those who arrived. As the RAF insisted on clear weather and bright moonlight, this was not a quite impossible task, but it would not have been easy, even for a highly skilled sleuth, and most of the people the Germans sent to do the work were not skilled at all. They were Parisian thugs, from the Bony-Lafont gang, run from a house in the Rue Lauriston by a former police inspector; they did not know much about country ways, and good agents fresh from Beaulieu had no trouble in outwitting them.

This was the company Harry Peulevé had to shrug off when a Lysander took him back to France – one of two that used the same field that night, 17–18 September 1943, but he took care to travel by himself[14] – to one of Déricourt's fields at Vieux-Briollay, close north-east of Angers. He detached himself with no difficulty from his would-be followers, and went down by train to Bordeaux, where his first set of contact addresses lay: there he found himself in hotter water still.

When he got to Bordeaux, he found the whole 'Scientist' circuit – as de Baissac's people were called in Baker Street – in a state of turmoil, brought on by the second-in-command in whose charge it had been left. This 'affaire Grandclément' was, like the 'affaire Hardy' or the 'affaire Déricourt', a considerable media sensation in post-war France, and as in the other two cases what really happened may never be cleared up. A few points are nevertheless certain.

André Grandclément was a personage of some standing in French politics and society, the son of an admiral, and a former aide-de-camp to the extreme right-winger, the *cagoulard* Colonel de la Rocque – who, though far to the right, was opposed to the Nazis because they were foreigners. Grandclément was brought into resistance in 1942 by his friend Marc O'Neil, and in the past year had done a great deal of work, mainly in the Bordelais, towards receiving parachute drops and hiding the arms they brought. He worked both with de Baissac, and with a large French body, the *Organisation Civile et Militaire* (OCM), that was composed mainly of retired officers like himself; he had risen already to colonel's rank in the army. His cover was that he was an insurance agent – this gave him excuses for travelling, and for having any number of socially unexpected acquaintances.

The scores of sorties by low-flying aircraft from Tempsford to south-western France attracted some German police attention. Simultaneously with the Gestapo's attack on F section's people in and around Paris at midsummer 1943, there were a few dozen arrests on suspicion in the Bordelais. One of those arrested mentioned Grandclément's address. The Germans raided his house. He was away, but they arrested his wife, and took away both a studio photograph of him, and a card index with a hundred names in it they found on his desk, marked 'potential policy-holders' but in fact containing, in clear, the particulars of a hundred fellow-resisters, none of whom were at once arrested. As a routine police measure, the photograph was circulated; a dutiful Gestapo officer recognized him from it in a Paris cafe, and arrested him on 19 September.

He was sent down to Bordeaux for interrogation, and there a particularly deft German operation persuaded him to change sides. He swallowed the familiar doctrine, 'Better Hitler than Stalin', and was disconcerted enough by the shock of arrest to come to believe that his primary duty as a good Frenchman was to oppose communism, wherever it was to be found. It was only a short step further to convince him that resistance was really working in the communist interest, and that therefore his duty was now to break up the clandestine network he had helped to create.

For a few hectic weeks, Grandclément was driven round the countryside in a Gestapo car, hunting arms dumps, while members of the circuit tried by telephone and bicycle to anticipate him and get the arms away to fresh hiding-places. Roger Landes, called 'Aristide', de Baissac's Gascon wireless operator and an uncommonly brave man, took huge risks in this connection. He survived to see most of the arms put to good use next summer, when resistance played an important part in clearing the Germans from the area. Grandclément was quietly assassinated in July 1944,[15] and Landes was abruptly ordered out of his own country by de Gaulle in September.[16]

What on earth, the reader will ask, have all these complications to do with Harry Peulevé? Simply this, that he walked unscathed through the worst of them. Like Marlborough's general, Cutts, who was nicknamed 'the Salamander' because he seemed to thrive where the fire was hottest, Peulevé seemed to have a private gift for survival, and even for calm, in trouble; a gift connected perhaps with his gift for hooding his personality, which was mentioned just now. He reached Bordeaux at the very worst moment of the 'affaire Grandclément', when the rates of flight and arrest were highest. He had to meet, in series, friends of de Baissac's, who would put him on to a whole group of further friends, waiting to be organized inland to the east.

This he did, quietly, unostentatiously, patiently; then he slipped away to get on with his own work. He could see that the Bordeaux circuit was in trouble, he was English enough to mind his own business, and French enough not to have the least difficulty in passing among the crowd, any more than in crossing the demarcation line.

De Baissac had had sharp words with Buckmaster about the area that Peulevé was going to open up, but was persuaded that it would really be absurd to try to run a secret organization so widespread that it had strongholds not only in Paris and in Bordeaux, but in the Corrèze as well. As it turned out, Landes's telegrams about the Grandclément affair so much agitated London that de Baissac was not then allowed back to the Bordelais at all, and transferred his circuit to south Normandy, where at the end of June 1944 he received an officer of my own brigade in the upper storey of a farmhouse which had a German battalion headquarters on the ground floor. But we must get back to Peulevé.

De Baissac, as a leading resister who had reliable touch with London and could therefore secure arms drops,[17] had been approached indirectly by the Malraux family, notable left-wingers who had built up some following in the departments of Corrèze, Dordogne and Lot, especially in the first of them. They wanted arms; if given arms, they promised action. Claude, Roland and Serge Malraux did most of the organizing; their half-brother André, already a world-famous novelist, provided money, prestige and occasional leadership.[18]

Besides the Malraux' grouping, Harry Peulevé found in the Corrèze a small, tightly knit, well-organized group of *Franc-Tireurs et Partisans* (FTP), whose leaders were communists, and in the Lot a larger, looser, equally eager body called the *Groupes Véni*, who were socialists. There were also still more numerous, and still more disparate, members of the OCM, socially and politically conservative, but informed about warfare. His task was to weld as many as he could of these resisters into trained, armed, disciplined groups and to carry out with them whatever tasks of ambush and sabotage seemed necessary to the Allied high command, in order to drive the Germans out of France.

Immediately, Harry's task was much simpler: it was to stay alive. The Corrèze was full already of tumult; both the FTP and the secret army of the OCM, misreading the course of the war, had come out prematurely into the hedgerows and started ambushing German cars and motor-cycles. A sparse and uncoordinated guerilla was already spluttering busily; strangers were liable to get short shrift. His adaptability, his indispensable clandestine connections – the addresses he had picked up in Bordeaux – and his calm nerves saved him.

Sharp German counter-attacks, shortages of arms and ammunition, and the onset of winter brought an armed truce to these troubled valleys by mid-November, and Peulevé could settle down to the business of organizing a new SOE circuit, called 'Author'.

He had his own wireless set, which saved him from one of the lasting sets of worries of a clandestine organizer. (Where is my operator? Is he or she safe? When and where exactly are we next in touch?) On the other hand, he had all the lasting worries of an operator's life on top of the busyness and the responsibility of running his own circuit. Sensibly, he did not go in for empire-building, that painfully common human failing; he saw early that the task Baker Street had set him was too big. 1944 was not a week old before a formidably competent pair of young Englishmen, George Hiller and Cyril Watney his wireless operator, parachuted in to take liaison with the *Groupes Véni* off his hands.

Both were severely wounded in action next summer, but not before they had done the work they were sent to do. Several thousand maquisards – young fighters living wild in the hills – armed by them and adhering to the *Groupes Véni* imposed telling delays on German armour trying to get to Normandy in mid-June, and kept the Lot valley humming till late August.[19]

Exactly the same sort of work was done that summer by Harry Peulevé's forces – it is hardly too much to call them his, though de Gaulle was the unseen chief to whom they looked – but he was not there to see. He had armed them and sorted them out into two effective blocs: the FTP and Malraux' adherents in one, about 1,500 strong, and the OCM and his personal following in the other, numbering over 2,000. Most of the arms were Sten sub-machine guns, and there was not a lot of ammunition, but there were plenty of grenades, a few Bren light machine guns, and an enormous amount of enthusiasm. This zeal was tempered with prudence, after the battles of the autumn.

The FTP groups, unaware that their strategy was in large part determined for them by the French communist party, took a more active part than most in patrolling, ambushing, and showing the red end of the tricolour prominently; the French communists being determined to do everything possible that might ease the Red Army's burden on the eastern front, no matter how severe the casualties elsewhere. The OCM followed de Gaulle's orders, and Peulevé himself those of the British chiefs of staff, as relayed through the staff hierarchy of SOE.

These led him personally to several parachute operations, in which he and a group of friends broke curfew to receive drops of arms, and hid them before dawn.[20] For these arms he held a lot of training classes, helped by Jacques Poirier whom the RAF parachuted in to help him. F section codenamed him, for a jest, 'Nestor' because he was so young. Poirier knew the area well, having fought in it and escaped from it before ever he met Peulevé, and had benefited greatly from SOE's security training. One of his best intelligence sources was his own father, a retired air force colonel; the rest of the circuit never knew till liberation that the two were father and son.[21]

Peulevé and Poirier believed in training by practical example, and in leading from the front, so they took part in a number of ambushes themselves, and soon got the local Germans exasperated. In early March 1944, for example, a German attempt to clear up a maquis encampment in the walnut forests round Montignac in the northern Dordogne cost the Germans over fifty dead, for light resistance casualties, in several hours' battle, fought almost in sight of the ruins of a castle that had been a key point in the Hundred Years' War against the English. (Unbeknown to any of the combatants, they were also within a couple of miles of the sacred caves of Lascaux. The sublime paintings there, accidentally discovered by two boys out rabbiting late in 1940, were hidden from everybody – even from the inquisitive Harry – by the sagacity of their schoolmaster and of the Abbé Breuil.[22])

The state of confusion, disarray and uncertainty to which resisters' work had reduced the neighbourhood by this time is eloquently spelt out in the diary of the newly appointed prefect of the Corrèze, Pierre Trouillé, who, though an official of the Vichy regime, was a secret sympathizer with resistance. Even in his own private office he found disloyalty to the regime; the simplest services of local government were no longer assured, and every man doubted every other.[23] This was fertile soil for insurrection, indeed minor insurrection seemed to break out every other week.

Maddeningly, within a fortnight of leading this successful action at Montignac, Peulevé fell by accident into German hands.

He lived in a house in a suburb of Brive. It was perhaps indiscreet of him to live in one place at all, and not to keep constantly on the move. At any rate, a near neighbour took a dislike to him – imagined, quite wrongly, that he was Jewish, and guessed, wrongly again, that he was a black marketeer, because he kept such odd hours. The neighbour tipped off the Gestapo, who happened to call at a moment when Peulevé and some friends were upstairs, transmitting a message to England.

They had not bothered to lock the front door. Harry himself had been on sentry duty at the window, but had moved over to the table where the transmitter was screwed down, to join in a discussion about tactics, thus not noticing when two large black cars drew up outside. He just had time to snatch up that day's messages and pop them in the stove, but there was the transmitter as manifest proof of guilt.

After the first torrent of blows and invective had died down, the Germans said 'Tell us who your organizer is. When do you next meet him?' 'Too bad,' Harry replied, 'I was to have met him a quarter of an hour ago. We always leave it that he gets in touch with me, not the other way round.' After prevaricating for some hours, he gave a description of a leading local collaborator, whom the Germans duly arrested, and held for a long time.

They held Harry even more firmly; after all, they had proof that he was a clandestine wireless operator, and after a few days he wisely claimed British officer status. As Captain Poole, he was sent to

Fresnes prison, just west of the present airport of Paris/Orly. Jacques Poirier took over his Corrèze circuit, with a new wireless operator dropped a few days later; the Germans suffered severely from it. Harry's spirits remained high, until in the crowded hall of Fresnes he caught sight, in a party of women prisoners being marched off for interrogation, of Violette Szabo.

He supposed security would keep them from exchanging more than agonized glances, till she waved to him cheerfully – she was an irrepressibly cheerful girl. He waved back; they were promptly swept off in different directions by their warders.

Pondering the confusions of the Fresnes entrance hall, Harry glimpsed a possibility of escape, and, being himself, he took it. Now and again he was taken, with a few random fellow-prisoners from Fresnes, to a fruitless cross-questioning at the *Sicherheitsdienst* office at 84–86 avenue Foch, near the Étoile. They travelled standing in separate steel compartments in a closed prison bus, and sharp-eyed SS sentries watched them in and out, covering them carefully with machine pistols. Once back inside Fresnes, there was more hugger-mugger: French warders, less alert, and more hanging about. One day they returned to Fresnes just at the moment when a mass of visitors, who had called on ordinary French criminal prisoners, were leaving; the main hall was crowded. At a moment when the warden in charge of his party was distracted, Peulevé unostentatiously joined the throng of visitors.

He ran promptly into a snag: on leaving, each visitor had to give up the chit that had given him or her permission to enter. He had a few sheets of lavatory paper in his jacket pocket, proffered one of them, and strolled on. Unluckily for him, the warder collecting the chits noticed, and called out. Peulevé broke into a run; a German sentry promptly shot him through the thigh and brought him down.

The sergeant of the guard ran up, recognized him, and had him carried back to his cell, where he was left quite alone. As no one came to look after his wound, he cared for himself; found that his thighbone was unbroken, and that the bullet was still lodged in his flesh, and dug it out with the only implement he had, the handle of his soup spoon. For the rest of his life he had a hole in his thigh, as wide as his little finger and a couple of inches deep; but the wound was quite clean, and promptly healed up. He was soon walking normally again, and was included in a large party, of some forty SOE agents, who were all sent together by train to Germany in mid-August 1944, a few days before the Germans abandoned Paris.

During the journey, he met Violette Szabo again: on a justly celebrated occasion. The train was under attack by the RAF. The guards fled to ditches beside the line. Violette, with another girl chained to her wrist, crawled along the train under fire – she was as irrepressibly brave as she was cheerful – distributing water to her fellow prisoners. That night the train stopped at Metz, and the prisoners were herded into some old barrack stables. He and Violette, each still chained to a companion, are supposed to have been able to talk through a chink in the woodwork.

Next day the women were sent off separately, to Ravensbrück. Harry never saw Violette again. The men found their way to Buchenwald.

Buchenwald concentration camp, built by a fearsome irony round an oak associated with Goethe, lies close to Weimar – so close indeed that the stench of Buchenwald's dead was clearly perceptible in Weimar market-place, in April 1945. (This was the moment when the general German cry was, 'We are as shocked as you are about these camps; we had no idea'.) It had been founded in 1937 by a group of 200 political prisoners, seven of whom survived. One of these seven has explained what it was, in a book which it would be an impertinence to seek to improve.[24] Equally there is no need to do more than refer the reader to an exceptionally thorough study of what the concentration camps were and what part they played in the Nazi system.[25] We shall have to revisit them later in this book, when we consider Pilecki's stay in Auschwitz, and can pass over Peulevé's stay quite briefly.

The new arrivals were held in Block 17, the normal starting-point, and tried to make some sense of the inferno. Fifteen of them were sent for by name, for some administrative purpose, the rest supposed. Poles in the crematorium squad disillusioned them; their fifteen friends had been executed.

A team of doctors and scientists in Block 50, devoted to medical experiments, conceived an escape scheme, which would work for three people at least. They chose Yeo-Thomas, the senior officer of the SOE group, who even in that company was an outstanding man,[26] and asked him to choose two more. He chose Stephane Hessel, a young Gaullist intelligence agent (later a French ambassador), and Harry Peulevé, because the two seemed to him the best qualified by character and physique for the ordeal to come. All – all! – the three of them had to do, was to take over the identity of a prisoner dying of typhus, who would die in the agent's name. Peulevé thus became Marcel Seigneur, a French gendarme whom he roughly resembled; but he had an extra narrow squeak. While Seigneur was in the closing throes of typhus, but still alive, Peulevé – as Poole – was called for on the camp loudspeaker, with another bunch of his companions for the chop. There was nothing to do but give him an injection to simulate typhus, which made him so ill that he ran a temperature of 41°C, and very nearly died anyhow. The SS proposed shooting him on a stretcher, but were too frightened of catching typhus themselves to dare to set foot in the hospital Block 46, where he lay. They sent a doctor over with a lethal injection instead; the doctor could not bring himself to inject a man he thought was dying anyhow, so Harry Peulevé survived.

By a great stroke of luck, it turned out to be fairly simple to pass as Seigneur, who had had no time to make friends in the camp close enough to notice changes in the details of his face and the timbre of his voice. After several weeks' companionship with SOE colleagues, who could share with him the knowledge that he was an Englishman and a former secret agent – points that had indeed become no secret to his captors, either – Peulevé/Seigneur was now again entirely on his own. Loss of companions he could bear; secrecy he could bear, he was good at it. The thing he found hardest to bear was the feeling that he had stolen Seigneur's life. In fact this was hardly so: Seigneur had died of a dangerous fever, in medical conditions pretty certain to be fatal to anybody.[27]

The change of identity released him from the exceptional watch the Germans kept on his colleagues: of 43 SOE agents sent to

Buchenwald, only seven survived. As a comparatively unimportant French prisoner, he got sent out of the main camp on working parties and from one of these he escaped, on 11 April 1945, by the simple expedient of running suddenly away. There were not enough guards to chase him without leaving the rest of the working party to escape as well.

By this time, Nazi Germany was breaking up altogether; the Allied armies were not far away. Peulevé stole some clothes from an abandoned farm, to hide his camp uniform, and walked west-wards. In a couple of days he had got within earshot of battle when, at a turn in a wood path, he bumped into a couple of Belgian SS. They asked for his papers; he had none. 'Shall we shoot him?' one asked the other – in French. At that moment an American army machine-gunner let off a burst, not far away. Peulevé pointed out that they would soon be the Americans' prisoners, and added some colourful details about what Americans would be likely to do to anyone they caught in SS uniform. 'All right', said one of the SS, 'we'll take your clothes'. All three started to undress. Peulevé picked up one of their pistols, and said 'Put your hands up. I am a British officer.' He tied their wrists behind them with their own belts, and covered them till they were overrun by United States troops a couple of hours later.

His two prisoners helped the bald-headed scarecrow to explain to the Americans which side he was on, and he quickly gave his name – Poole – and got himself flown back to England, where Vera Atkins of F section received him, looked after him, put him back in touch with his horrified family, and began to get his story out of him.

Though he had escaped from Buchenwald, he never recovered from it; it haunted his dreams for the rest of his life, as it haunts the other survivors still. He had seen humanity at its very worst, for months on end. Kogon, it is true, stood it for more years than he had to stand it for months: clearly, with even greater inner resources of will. No one who passed through it was ever the same again.

Nor could anyone who had not been there, as a prisoner, really take in quite how frightful it had been. Everyone was kind and cheerful and congratulatory; he had medals and decorations, British

71

and French; he tried to rest. Yet he could not forget, so he could not rest.

His superiors in SOE praised him very highly, and made sure he got a job. He landed in fact a good responsible job, with the great Shell oil company, that used his French and gave him plenty of chances to travel in the Mediterranean and the Caribbean. He still could not settle to anything.

He had a short, happy marriage to a Danish girl, Marie-Louise John. They married in Tunis in 1952, and she bore him a daughter and a son; for a while he was serene. But his sleep was never secure from nightmares about captivity; the cruelties of Buchenwald had bitten too deep for him to rest. Before long, his wife found she could not hold him to any single house or city. She went back to Denmark with the children, and divorced him for desertion.[28]

This cast him down, and he found work for Shell more and more irksome in its calls on his time and his responsibilities. On an impulse he gave it up, and moved to an Oxfordshire firm called Handy Angles, becoming their overseas manager for western Europe. This involved plenty of travelling, which he enjoyed; though late in the evenings, when he had had a few drinks, he developed a tendency to become quarrelsome with other men, total strangers whom he accused of being SS in disguise, come to persecute him.

Not long before he died, he told his sister that he had lost all zest for the world, and did not want to live any more. On 18 March 1963 he arrived in Seville by car after nearly two days' continuous driving, through from northern Italy. Over a drink before dinner, he remarked that he was tired, and would go to bed early without bothering to dine. He went up to his hotel room, typed a brief report for Handy Angles, felt unwell, lay down on the bed, and died peacefully of a heart attack.

He is buried in Seville. His first girlfriend (who married a Barnardo's boy) went there to lay flowers on his grave.

5

Victor Gerson

Haim Victor Gerson was born at Southport in Lancashire in 1896, the son of a Levantine textile merchant who thought Lancashire a good base for his work. Southport was in those days a small, quiet bathing resort, with plenty of sand dunes for children to play in, and farming country on the inland side. It lies twenty miles north of Liverpool, then as now a great port, and forty miles north-west of Manchester, where the Royal Exchange was then the commercial capital of the world. Round Manchester lay a dozen busy and prosperous cotton towns. In it the cricket ground of Old Trafford was already famous; and C.P. Scott, editor of the *Manchester Guardian* in its golden age, had the ear of leading cabinet ministers from the end of 1905. All seemed to be for the best in the best of all possible worlds, if one had money, and the Gersons were not poor.

As members of the Anglo-Jewish community, they were somewhat remote from the ruling class of Edwardian England, which still consisted mainly of the old landed gentry and the Oxford- and Cambridge-trained intelligentsia. They knew that they were firmly fixed on the commercial side of the great gulf that was then still supposed to divide gentlefolk from 'trade'. Young Victor was brought up all the same to behave as a gentleman: to be straight with everybody, always to tell the truth, to honour his parents, be generous and work hard.

Ever since Anglo-Saxon and feudal times, the gentry had been aware of their duty to bear arms in defence of their country, and his upper-class contemporaries learned to shoot, to ride and to command almost as automatically as they learned to read and write and to stand up when a lady entered the room. In an age of which two of the upper classes' unspoken mottoes were 'It will last out my time' and 'Everyone knows his place', there was not much mobility between classes. Victor Gerson cherished no wild hopes, got on smoothly with his parents and his school friends, and looked stronger and older than his equals in age.

This was an advantage to him in the summer of 1914, when what his generation came to call the Great War broke out. An obscure group of Serb student revolutionaries succeeded at the second attempt at killing the heir to the Habsburg throne, the Archduke Franz Ferdinand, when he had the temerity to visit Sarajevo, the mediaeval capital of Serbia, on the 525th anniversary of a great Serbian defeat – Balkan peoples have memories as long as the Irish – on 28 June. After a month's dithering by the Habsburg government of Austria-Hungary, that country forced war on Serbia late in July. The Russians ordered mobilization, in case they had to protect their Serb cousins, whereupon the Germans, to protect their Austrian cousins, declared war on Russia. They had only one war plan ready, which involved defeating Russia's ally France first, so they declared war on France as well.

Up to this point, British financial and commercial leaders were all appalled at what was going on, and overwhelmingly anxious that Great Britain should remain neutral; a doctrine the *Manchester Guardian* was advocating on Saturday, 1 August, the day of the German declaration of war on Russia. On the brink of the holiday weekend, everything changed. The Germans' war plan carried with it an immediate invasion of Belgium, guaranteed neutral since 1839 by all the great powers of Europe. To defend that guarantee, Great Britain declared war on Germany on 4 August; even C.P. Scott approved.

All over combatant Europe, in defiance of the Socialist International's plan for stopping any war by a general strike, there was a great surge of patriotic enthusiasm. Conscripts marched off garlanded to war, through cheering crowds; and in Great Britain, where there was no conscription, young men crowded the recruiting offices. Young Gerson joined them, no questions asked about his age, and found himself a private in the King's Liverpool Regiment, the eighth regiment of the line.

It was an excellent regiment, formed under James II, distinguished under Marlborough and since; it sent thirty battalions into combat this time. He had a heavy war, most of it in France; he was promoted corporal in 1916, and in that rank went all through the murderous Battle of the Somme. Late in November 1916, an order reached his company: Corporal Gerson, H.V., was to report forthwith to Railway Transport Officer, Victoria. He did not wait for a second invitation. When he got to London, RTO Victoria looked askance at the chalk mud on his kit, but handed him a first-class warrant to Crowborough, where he was met at the station, driven to a large country house, and slept – for the first time for months – in a bed with sheets.

Next morning, after an excellent breakfast, he was told that he was to be trained as a spy – 'You do speak Turkish, don't you?' – unless he had any objection; anything was better than the trenches, he had none. But his prospective employers, it turned out, did. On discovering that his father was still a Turkish, and so an enemy, national, they had Gerson reduced to the ranks and sent back to France as a private in the labour corps. He spent the next two years filling sandbags at the great base camp at Étaples.

This ludicrous posting saved his life: not a single one of his companions in that King's Liverpool Regiment company on the Somme survived the fighting at Passchendaele in the late summer of 1917.

When the war was over he had had enough of England for the time being and settled in Paris, though retaining the British nationality of his birth. He bought a flat at 60 rue de Lisbonne, round the corner from the Rue de Berne immortalized by Manet, in a quiet and respectable district of bourgeois Paris above the Gare Saint-Lazare, and became known as a dealer in fine rugs and carpets. He had a singularly happy marriage till his wife fell ill and died, in the late 1930s, and their only child, a boy, was killed in a motor-cycle accident at seventeen.

Gerson was severely shaken, but not shattered, by this double tragedy and shortly before the next great war began, he was married again, to Giliana Balmaceda, a strikingly beautiful young Chilean actress who brought plenty of colour into his life. She brought it into his flat as well: she kept parakeets and other exotic birds behind a golden grille in the drawing room.

At the exodus in the second week of June 1940, the Gersons fled west like their neighbours and managed to get clear away to England, where they looked round for ways to help in the war. In the course of their journeyings across western France, Madame Gerson secured a visa on her unexpired Chilean passport, in her maiden name, allowing her to visit Vichy France. This soon turned out useful.

Gerson happened to have met in Paris a quiet-spoken Englishman called Leslie Humphreys, who was there on behalf of one of SOE's forerunners, the formerly mysterious Section D;[1] and who became, when SOE was founded, the first head of F, its independent French section. Humphreys and the Gersons regained touch with each other in London in the autumn of 1940, and Humphreys realized that Victor Gerson was just the sort of man who could be of vast use to SOE's work – if he could be persuaded to join it. Chance in fact provided an opening for Giliana, before there was one for Victor.

SOE spent the first year of its existence, from its creation by a war cabinet decision in mid-July 1940, fighting to get itself accepted as an integral part of the war machine among other departments – some of them not much older – in which intrusions of any kind were resented. Frightful bureaucratic squabbles need not detain us here, but one result we do need to notice.

SOE was starved of such little news as there was, about what was actually going on on the continent. To anybody of enterprise, this presented a simple challenge: someone must go across to find out. More, much more easily said than done; but Madame Gerson's Chilean passport provided an opening. Humphreys briefed her with great care and precision about what he wanted to know, and she set off on a task that extended her capacities as an actress to the full. Travelling without a companion, or even a wedding ring, by such ordinary steam and rail lines as she could find, she went through

Portugal and Spain into southern France, reaching Vichy, after an exasperating journey of several weeks, late in May 1941. This makes her, by fourteen months, the earliest of SOE's women agents to visit France, indeed she only arrived about a fortnight after F section's very first parties of parachutists, who had landed near Châteauroux in the second week of May to start the work of subversion.[2]

She must have had a tedious time; the task of a secret agent at work, even when the agent is a beautiful girl in her twenties, is usually a great deal duller than readers of spy thrillers might imagine, and Giliana Gerson's task was duller than most. A great deal of her time was spent waiting about, in bars and stations and hotel lounges and town halls, queuing and listening, finding out how people lived. In mid-June she came out of France again, southward by train, bringing with her something SOE's forgery section had been longing to get hold of – a set of current Vichy French food and tobacco ration cards – and a lot of simple, basic news: train timetables, bus time-tables, rules about booking seats on trains, curfew rules, rules about what papers one had to carry, food prices, stamp prices, availability of taxis, drinks, and telephone boxes, prices of clothes and shoes – of which, as of food, scarcity had already begun. She was in Lisbon by the end of June but, having no high priority, had to wait ten weeks more before she could reach England; she was not available for detailed cross-questioning in London till 24 August.

This made her married life no more easy, for her husband was standing by to go to France at the next change of moon. They had hardly had time to see each other before he was dropped, on the night of 6–7 September, to a reception committee formed from F section's advance party near Châteauroux.[3] He went in a party of six, the largest drop SOE made into France till 1943, when it knew its business better. His companions included two of the section's stars, Ben Cowburn on a prolonged reconnaissance of oil targets, and Michael Trotobas after whom the rue du Capitaine Michel at Lille is named. But F section's history has been written elsewhere, from a number of different angles: we must stay with Victor Gerson.

His cover, of textile merchant, gave him no trouble, nor did passing as a Frenchman, after nearly twenty years' residence in Paris.

77

His perfect French did retain a light trace of English accent. In high French society this has often been an acceptable quirk, and nobody noticed or minded it in the commercial world he moved in in the thirties and forties. (By compensation, his perfect English retained a just perceptible French undertone.) His tasks were to make various inquiries for Humphreys in Lyons and Marseilles, and, if he saw fit, to launch a small subversive network in either.

A few days in Lyons convinced him that for the time being there was nothing he could usefully do there: he took a train for Marseilles. There, through an SOE contact, he was pressingly invited to call at the Villa des Bois, on the smartest outskirts of the port.

The contact systems that SOE had so far developed were still very much at the rudimentary stage: the sort of tradecraft about danger signals, passwords, fallback appointments that seems second nature to a Le Carré agent was all but unknown to its people. Gerson nevertheless had what one might call a flair for this work and he – alone of his colleagues who got the invitation – made one or two inquiries about the Villa des Bois before presenting himself there. The answers led to more questions and the more he heard, the less he liked the prospect. When he proved unable to reach any of his friends who had already been to the Villa, at any other address, he decided – correctly, it turned out long afterwards – that the Villa was a trap, manned by anti-British Vichy police. He still had some money left, so he took a train to Perpignan, bought the services of a reliable smuggler, and was in Barcelona before Christmas.

He reported to Humphreys when he returned to London, and found that staff arrangements had changed while he was away. F section had a new head, H.R. Marriott, formerly of Courtauld's, and Humphreys now bore a new set of tasks as head of a separate section, called DF. DF's job was to establish and maintain escape lines, all over Europe west of Germany, along which SOE's agents could travel easily and fast. Humphrey's sceptical wisdom and Gerson's clandestine flair between them made DF into one of SOE's minor triumphs. It has not had much publicity – both of them loathed publicity; it did rather well.

Victor Gerson went back to France on his second mission on 21

April 1942, travelling to the Riviera coast by submarine, in a good deal of discomfort, with a Breton taxi-driver called Marcel Clech, an F section wireless operator who had been trying to get to France for eighteen months. They were taken ashore, separately, by canoe by Peter Churchill, an expert at this task. Gerson, like Peulevé, kept well clear of such contacts as Churchill was able to offer ashore. He went to Lyons, and settled down to the serious business of clandestinity.

He formed the core of his circuit, which London called the 'Vic' line, from friends in the Lyonnais Jewish community, choosing those who were Jewish by descent, because they would already have had some practice in keeping themselves discreetly apart from the mainstream of ordinary life round them, but avoiding those who were ostentatiously Jewish in manners, appearance or religion, because they would be too conspicuous. Besides, there had been a good deal of anti-semitism in the France of the just-vanished Third Republic, and the Vichy regime was not above currying favour with the Germans by indulging in some anti-semitic activity itself. Over 60,000 Jews were deported eastward from France during the war, of whom only 2,800 returned: not the proudest page in French or in German history.[4]

The worst phase of persecution for Jews in France broke out later that summer. It weighed harder on foreign Jews than on French ones, and harder on the poor than on the wealthy; Gerson's circuit survived it with no serious trouble. The circuit had three nodal points: in Lyons, supervised by George Levin, in Paris under Levin's friend Jacques Mitterand (brother of a future president), and in Perpignan where Gerson made the crucial arrangements himself. At Lyons, Levin worked with two brothers called Racheline and with two married sisters, Mme Levêque and Mme Carnadelle. Mme Levêque ran a fashionable women's hairdressing establishment, and this shop became a sort of hub round which the circuit revolved. A hairdresser's served splendidly for this purpose – plenty of comings and goings, constantly changing faces, ample opportunities for hiding-places and disguises. It had one disadvantage: it was fixed to a single spot.

In Paris, Mitterand sought out safe houses; places where travellers down the line could live inconspicuously for days or if necessary weeks, while arrangements were being made for moving them farther. The former and future capital, with its long forbidding streets of tall stone houses already divided into separate apartments, was also ideal for the task, if trouble enough was taken, as Mitterand took it, to discover reliable safe-house-keepers and – equally important – reliable concierges.

The Perpignan end was the most tricky. Here Gerson had a particularly lucky find: a young Spanish anarchist general called Revira, who used the cover name of 'Martin', had already arranged a set of reliable routes and guides over the eastern Pyrenees. 'Martin' had meant these to serve the purposes of the defeated Spanish republic; he was a good enough democrat and a keen enough anti-fascist to see that the war had put the British on the same side as the Spanish republicans, vis-à-vis Hitler and Pétain if not vis-à-vis France.

He and Gerson cooperated long and usefully, and he also got on well with one of Gerson's leading helpers in Lyons and Perpignan, Thérèse Mitrani ('Denise'). 'Vic' was a lodger in 'Denise's' house for quite a lot of this mission, and the presence of her six-year-old son[5] may have helped him to form one of his line's strictest rules: *no children in safe houses*.

It will give a clearer idea of how his line worked to quote a whole set of these rules, as Jacques Mitterand recollected them in February 1945:

- Members were only known and referred to by their pseudonyms.
- Domiciles of the regular staff of the Circuit always remained secret.
- New members of the Organization had to drop all previous clandestine activities.
- All regular members had to sever contact with their families, and [move house from] where they had lived before being in the Circuit.
- It was strictly forbidden to carry any papers giving names of contacts, or addresses.

- Verbal messages between Informant and Organizer through couriers were always given in veiled language which couriers could not understand.
  [Alternatively,]
- When messages could not be put in veiled language or could not be remembered by the courier, it would be written on thin tissue paper, inserted into a cigarette, or carried in such a way that it could easily be eaten or dropped.
- Passwords had to be given, word perfect, otherwise they would not be accepted.
- Bodies in safe houses were not allowed to go out at any time under any circumstances [except of course when it was time to move on].
- Members were warned never to call on any safe house:, without first checking the security of the house by telephone.[6]

As the French and the German police were both quite likely to listen to telephone calls at random, there was also a whole series of simple telephone codes, as well as lists of banned meeting-places, such as all Paris bars and cafés. Levin added a further rule: 'When carrying incriminating documents – accomplish the clandestine mission forthwith before any personal or innocent work.'

Those of course were the rules that applied when the line was at its best, after everyone in it had acquired plenty of experience. It began more roughly. Some of its earliest passengers complained that 'Martin's' guides at the Pyrenean end, in particular, looked too much like conspirators, and might thus endanger their charges. Humphreys passed the warning back to Gerson, who soon made sure there was no ground for that complaint.

The line's first major operation was a classic of escape, and one in which Gerson the more willingly took part, because most of the people it rescued had been caught at the Villa des Bois, from which he had managed to keep clear. All these prisoners – there were several more, besides the unlucky companions who had jumped with him in October – spent a horrible winter in Périgueux jail. Their main consolation was that at least they were still in French hands, and had not been handed over to the Germans; Périgueux was still in unoccupied France, where the Gestapo was already influential, but not yet dominant. A lesser, but still important, relief came from the fact that one of them – Jean-Pierre Bloch, a former radical senator – happened to have a wife who lived not too far away. Gaby Bloch's food parcels mitigated the worst horrors of prison diet.

In the spring of 1942 the whole party was moved out of prison, after representations made by the American diplomatic staff at Vichy, into less cramped – but still highly disagreeable – quarters, in the concentration camp at Mauzac, also in the department of the Dordogne. French concentration camps are now nearly forgotten, but no one who has read Arthur Koestler's *Scum of the Earth*[7] will ever be able to forget them altogether. They lacked the intense will to evil, and the apparatus for mass killing, that have made the German camps unforgettable; but rest camps they were not.

They did have, though, one huge advantage over the fortress-like gaol: escape from them was thinkable. Through Gaby Bloch, the party got in touch with Virginia Hall, an American journalist, who was F section's imperturbable fender-off of troubles in Lyons; she in turn got in touch with Gerson. The dozen would-be escapers were all in the same hut; they all had a good look at the key; Georges Bégué, F section's first wireless operator, manufactured a duplicate, and – with money sent in by Madame Bloch – bought a guard. Michael Trotobas looked after crossing the wire and avoiding the sentries. At 3 a.m. on 16 July, a prearranged night, they all crept out. Gerson had a lorry waiting for them over the hill, and a rough wood-land lodging twenty miles away. Albert Rigoulet ('Le Frisé' – 'Curly') who drove the lorry, had helped to receive the 'Corsican' mission nine months before. The Racheline brothers shepherded the escapers, by twos and threes, to Lyons, whence they were fed on to 'Martin's' routes, and so away.

Several of them had important parts to play in the secret war: such as Trotobas and Robert Lyon as scourges of the railway system,[8] Bégué as F section's signal officer, George Langelaan (another American reporter) on propaganda work,[9] or Philippe Liewer, the organizer for whom Violette Szabo acted as courier. There cannot often have been an escape so rich in promising material.

Gerson himself returned to England, down his own line as a matter of course, as soon as he was satisfied that everybody who had got away from Mauzac was safely stowed, and that there were no dangers of reprisal. Yet as Humphreys was quick to explain to him, the Mauzac affair was a more conspicuous business than the steady, unostentatious, beavering that DF section required of him.

For the regular maintenance, year in year out, of a permanently open underground railway across France into Spain, they devised two extra refinements: a system, known technically as a chain of cut-out rendezvous, that kept the segments of the line separated from each other and a system also for security's sake of parallel lines, with no connection between them, only one of which was to be in use at a time.

The business of cut-out rendezvous looked complicated enough from an escaper's point of view, but was in fact fairly straightforward. The escaper, equipped with forged papers to support a false identity – no easy task, but not one about which much is published, even yet – is taken by a guide, usually a demurely dressed young woman, for a walk. At some public spot, not too remote and not too crowded, she parts with him, ideally leaving him seated on a park bench. He simply sits. Ten or fifteen minutes later, a total stranger approaches and offers him a simple prearranged password, such as 'Do you happen to have any matches on you?' This is his next guide, with whom he sets out on the next stage of the journey. The guides never meet; they get in touch with each other, through a further set of cut-outs, by telephone messages, signals in shop-window displays, and so on. If either guide is arrested, she cannot give the other away; neither has any idea of the other's identity or appearance.

The nub of this system lay as much in patience and discipline on the travellers' part, as in care and caution on the guides'. If the guides were not careful and cautious, they would not be likely to be in Gerson's employ, and if the travelling agents were not patient and disciplined, they had no business to be in SOE.

Parallel lines, again, called for care, calm, and discipline; without rock-hard nerves, no escape line could run at all. Gerson, on Humphreys' advice, first doubled up all his arrangements, and then tripled them, so that, everywhere along his routes, there were two dormant alternative lines ready to spring into action, without notice, at the sound of a telephone delivering a code word. All that the people who were to run them had to do was to preserve the even tenor of their ways, hugging quietly to themselves the knowledge of their secret task, and never doing anything to suggest to any neighbour or acquaintance that they were at all out of the ordinary.

Couriers, message-carriers, guides, safe-house-keepers in all three of these lines were exempt from the rule that governed the lives of Gerson himself, the Racheline brothers, Levin, Mitterand and any wireless operators they might have: an automatic change of name, address and personality, at least once every three months. Thanks to this elaborate series of safety precautions, the circuit survived three penetrations (due to no fault of its own) by the Gestapo, in June and October 1943 and early in 1944; not without casualties, but quite without any impact on its proper work, passing SOE's agents round western Europe.

What held the circuit together, as a working organism, beyond its members' love of France and hatred of Nazi oppression, was the quiet strength of its commander's personality. Not many people who worked for him knew him even by sight; he knew a good many more of them, by sight and by pseudonym at least. His own pseudonym of 'Vic' became known all down the line; so did some of his rules about how to behave, and nobody in it, in that rather more orderly society than our own, wanted to do anything of which 'Vic' was known to disapprove.

Beyond exerting this rather odd form of command, what did he do? He travelled a good deal – consonantly with his usual covers, as one sort of textile merchant or another. After his initial 'Vic' mission (April–August 1942) and some lengthy consultations with DF staff, he returned to France by parachute late in 1942 for an eight-month stay, entirely taken up with setting up his second and third lines, and testing them,[10] and surviving the Gestapo's first attack.

On the night of 19–20 August 1943 he was brought out of France by an RAF light bomber, which spent a few minutes under Déricourt's supervision on a hilltop north of Angers. A party of ten agents, shepherded down from Paris by Déricourt's friends and shadowed in addition by the usual French gangsters, had a horribly uncomfortable brief spell in the moonlight, because their grassy hilltop happened that night to have a herd of bullocks pastured on it. The beasts panicked at the noise of the aircraft's approach and stampeded to and fro in a frantic herd: one of the prospective passengers, who had already spent many months in acutely dangerous clandestinity and was to spend many more, recollects it as the worst fright of his life.[11] Luckily, they were nowhere near the aircraft while it was on the ground, and happened not to trample on any of the passengers either.

Gerson had a busy autumn. He was soon dropped back into France again, visited Barcelona in October – missing another Gestapo incursion into his line – and then came out once more through Spain to London. On 15–16 November he again visited the impromptu airfield near Angers, being put into France from a Hudson in what the pilot innocently described as 'a very straightforward operation'. Ten F agents were lifted off, four more arrived with 'Vic'. All these four were arrested by the German security authorities, three of them that very night. Déricourt was paid £20,000 of Gestapo money in return for them, having provided the Germans even more lavishly than usual with all the details. He would have got £25,000 had the Germans captured 'Vic' as well; but Gerson was too old a hand to be caught by a Parisian gangster. He took the usual sensible man's precautions to make sure he was not being followed; avoided the train to Paris, which the others took and quietly picked up the threads of his circuit at Lyons.

Apart from one more brief trip across the Pyrenees to England next month, and an uneventful return by parachute early in 1944, he was in France until its liberation; mainly in Lyons and Perpignan; always on the watch; often on the move. Once, when travelling by train between Paris and Lyons with Levin, he was arrested on suspicion, as was his companion. Both were respectably, even smartly dressed, they were travelling first-class, and they stuck with such perfect aplomb to their cover stories, which made it inconceivable that any police force should need to talk to such entirely innocent business men, that they were at once released. They were more fortunate than some of their subordinates, who fell into German hands in circumstances that left little room for doubt.

The German Abwehr colonel in charge of the German forces' security in the Netherlands, a highly efficient policeman called Giskes, had succeeded in every intelligence officer's dream: he had captured, in March 1942, an SOE wireless operator with his set, and had managed to take almost entire control, for a while, of SOE's work in his area.[12] This feat had a good deal of publicity in the 1950s; the fact that it was outclassed by the British security services, which ran for much longer the entire German espionage and sabotage effort in Great Britain, remained secret for nearly twenty years longer.[13]

SOE's N section, supposed to be operating into the Netherlands, eventually grew restive, and arranged for some of its agents to come back to this country. DF provided a point of contact with 'Vic', and four young men travelled down the line together in midsummer 1943. Two of them broke the circuit's rules in Lyons, and insisted on going out for an evening's drinking; they were given, in his own words, 'a very stiff security lecture' by 'Vic' himself, for endangering everybody's safety by their carelessness. He let all four of them go on all the same, to Perpignan whence they left for the Pyrenees, concealed behind piles of crates in a greengrocer's lorry. At a deserted spot near the foothills the lorry was unexpectedly stopped and searched; the four men were found. They went quietly. Well they might, for they were Gestapo agents, and their arrest was prearranged.

The lorry-driver got away with the improbable story that he did not know he had passengers on board, and was released. Gerson, wrongly suspecting he might be a German agent, did not re-employ him, and at once moved everybody, himself included, with whom the four had come into contact, so that no further arrests resulted.

Two earlier bogus Dutchmen had turned up in Paris in May, when they had easily stepped straight into the middle of F section's big but insecure 'Prosper' circuit. Again, a prearranged 'arrest' took place, under the noses of some members of 'Prosper'. That circuit did not last much longer.[14]

One of these two bogus Dutchmen, an Alsace-born ex-Foreign legionary called Richard Christmann, reappeared in Paris in October 1943, this time accompanying a real N section agent called van Schelle ('Apollo'), who had been shot down on his way into Holland and believed his companion to be a genuine resister. Christmann and van Schelle travelled down the 'Vic' line as far as Lyons, while 'Vic' himself happened to be on his flying visit to Barcelona.

DF and Gerson were both suspicious of Christmann, who was separated from van Schelle; the latter was safely and promptly brought out through Spain. Christmann, cross-questioned by Levin, spun an elaborate story about diamond-smuggling which necessitated – he said – his personal appearance on the Dutch frontier in a few days' time, and vanished.

He went back to The Hague, where he was an assistant to Giskes, and the slow machine of the German police bureaucracy ground over his reports. The machine, though slow, was thorough, as were the reports, for Christmann was an observant policeman, and had more idea than most escape line passengers of what was going on round him and of where he was. On 21 January 1944 the Germans struck: they arrested the safe-house-keepers with whom he had stayed in Paris in May and in October, and two other Parisian families in the circuit, and the girl courier who had accompanied him to Lyons, and, worst, a week later, Madame Levêque the hairdresser. Levin they missed, and Mitterand, and Gerson, because all three had moved.

This was the solitary point at which Gerson made anything that even the meticulous Humphreys would have classified as a slip. When first starting up his line, he had made some use of Paris friends he knew from before the war. By some unhappy admission, made by a prisoner in German hands who knew the truth, the Germans became aware that he was working in French resistance somewhere, and knew his home address, which was no secret. They thought it probable that he would call, sooner or later, at his own home; home was a steady magnet that drew resisters back from the odd, if not exotic lives they led to the world that was utterly familiar, the world of peace. There were several cases of Frenchmen, Norwegians or other exiles sent back for secret work into their own countries, who made straight for their parents' or their wives' homes, because the strain of living under a false identity was more than they could stand. Gerson was made of a different fibre; he took care to resist the temptation to move among his own belongings, even for a few familiar moments. The one magnet that might conceivably have drawn him, his wife, was not there. For months the Germans kept watch on 60 rue de Lisbonne: no trace of Vic. Eventually, they requisitioned the apartment and a couple of secret policemen moved in. It was a comfortable flat, well furnished and conveniently placed, and suited them nicely. They liked it so much that when they left in August 1944, contrary to the then usual German forces' practice they did not pillage the place. When Vic came home next month, he found that even the prints of British army uniforms on his study wall were undefaced and undisturbed. Giliana had only one thing to lament: the parakeets' grille was broken and all her birds were dead.

It turned out, alas, that her marriage was dead also. The strains of danger and separation had been too much for both of them, and the tides of war had driven them too far apart for a new start with each other to be possible. They parted in the winter of 1944–5; each happily remarried, she to an eminent Chilean diplomat, he to a mannequin who had spent a gentle war in Paris fending off the attentions of German officers.

'Vic' kept on the flat at 60 rue de Lisbonne, but did not live there all the time; he resumed business as a dealer in fine carpets. Once, some twenty-five years after the liberation, I was having a drink with him on a pavement in the Champs Elysées, and asked him whether he thought his curious career as a secret travel agent had been worth while. 'Look round you,' he said, 'is there a uniform in sight?'

6

Andrée de Jongh

There was a degree of deliberation about the Vic line; it had a tone of calm, colourless security about it, as might be expected of an offshoot of a service that had to exist and to act in particular secrecy. Let us turn now to an escape line that ran with more spontaneity; with equal devotion; and, as far the numbers carried along it went, with even more success. In this kind of war, spontaneity and success are often forerunners of tragedy; tragedy was held off this line for a while by boundless high spirits, accompanied by almost boundless good fortune.

Its founder and inspirer was an exact contemporary of Peulevé's, and a whole generation younger than Gerson; she was still in the cradle when he was fighting on the Somme. Andrée was the second daughter of Frédéric de Jongh, who became headmaster of a primary school in Schaerbeek, the area of Brussels that lies between the old city centre and the park and palace of Laeken. She thus came from a background comparable in some ways to Moulin's, with similar intellectual and anti-clerical traditions round her from her early years, but there were important differences as well. She was born and grew up in a large city; until she had learned to walk and to talk, the city she lived in was under enemy occupation in wartime; her early childhood was necessarily therefore much more restricted, as well as physically less sunny, than his had been. And primary schools in industrial suburbs, vitally important though they are, do not as a rule have the contacts with the great world that may fall to professors in cities.

An extra childhood influence gave her an early and permanent leaning towards resistance. Not far from the time she was conceived, Edith Cavell, an English nurse who had stayed behind to work in Brussels when the Germans invaded, was shot dead by them after trial on 12 October 1915, for having helped some six hundred British soldiers, many of whom she had hidden in her house or her hospital, to escape into Holland, then neutral. It is now publicly known that Miss Cavell had been a spy as well as an escape line organizer; it is unclear whether the Germans were aware of this.[1] If they were, it may help to account for their refusal to listen to the many attempts made by neutral diplomats to save her life; in those days shooting a lady was regarded as exceptionally base, and the act turned out a propaganda gift for Germany's enemies.

Frédéric de Jongh was a tremendous admirer of Miss Cavell's escape work, and never ceased to preach it to his daughters as an example of noble conduct. Her words the night before she died, 'Standing as I do in view of God and Eternity, I realise that patriotism is not enough.[2] I must have no bitterness towards anyone', rang often in the ears of Suzanne and Andrée de Jongh. It was part of the humanist creed of love for their fellow creatures, in which they were brought up.

Their father's views were wide enough to include clerical as well as lay heroic figures. Someone else Andrée greatly admired, from childhood, was Father Damien, the Belgian peasant boy who took his sick brother's place in a mission to the South Seas, devoted himself to the leper colony at Molokai in the Hawaiian islands and died of leprosy himself in 1889. Ill-founded rumours after his death triggered off a magnificent pamphlet by R. L. Stevenson,[3] and woke the world of charity up to the need to combat leprosy on a world scale; a battle not yet quite over.

Even as a small child, Andrée de Jongh showed plenty of energy and spirit, and a will of her own; her nickname in the family was 'little cyclone'.[4] She and her father recognized that she was no intellectual giant, but she had distinct gifts for drawing. She also, anxious to follow where her conscience led her, took some evening courses in first aid in a Brussels hospital. When she grew up, she got a job as a commercial artist with Sofina, the great property combine.

She was something of a perfectionist, but no sort of prig; she was slim, strong, lively, humorous, energetic; she radiated cheerfulness and good spirits, and was an excellent companion. She was also, with a neat figure, fair hair, and striking blue eyes, far from plain. Her somewhat more conventional sister Suzanne got married, though in an unconventional way, to Paul Wittek, a refugee orientalist from Austria who was a widower with three small children. Andrée remained single, for none of the young men she met quite came up to her standards of what a life's companion ought to be.

When the war came again to Belgium, suddenly, on 10 May 1940, she was working at Malmédy, close to the German border, in a town that had indeed been a part of Prussian Germany before 1919 when a plebiscite had transferred it to Belgium. She threw up her job at once and went back to Brussels, knowing that in wartime nurses would be needed; there were plenty of wounded to look after. Her parents were delighted to have her back in their Schaerbeek house, which by now they shared with the Witteks and with other lodgers; she did not stay there very long. Paul Wittek bolted westwards at once, knowing the Nazis would have no soft treatment for him if they caught him. He reached England eventually, was interned for a few weeks as a matter of routine, and was then able to join the anti-Nazi propaganda war.

Much of the pattern of Andrée's earliest childhood now repeated itself: jackboots on the pavements of Brussels; a sullen and resentful population; an active underground press; food rationing and food shortage; a noisy group of profiteers, doing nicely out of the occupation and not much caring who knew it; some devoted people – in a few cases, identically the same people in both wars – working in secret to provide intelligence about what the Germans were up to; and a lot of Allied soldiers in hiding. The military context was quite different, and so was the political one. In the 1914 war, a Belgian army had remained on Belgian soil, at the westernmost extremity of the country, where the 400-mile-long trench line of the western front – originating at the Swiss end of Alsace – reached the sea. This time the nearest Belgian troops were exiles in Great Britain and the Belgian government-in-exile settled there with them, in London. King Albert had commanded his army in the field; King Leopold III thought he should share the sufferings of his people, and spent the war a virtual prisoner in Laeken, till he was transported to Germany in 1944.

Andrée de Jongh found herself, in fact, in a setting which gave her a chance to emulate Edith Cavell, the heroine of her girlhood; the prospect that she might share Miss Cavell's fate did not deter her from what she saw to be her duty.

Being a sensible girl, she began cautiously and carefully. She moved from one temporary hospital job to another, in Brussels and Bruges, finding out where there were British or Belgian wounded who might want to escape when their wounds allowed. For a time she worked under the orders of one of Miss Cavell's own former assistants, Mlle Bihet,[5] in Brussels, both at that moment confining themselves strictly to nursing. Several times Andrée made herself helpful to wounded British prisoners, assisting them to send reassuring notes to their families through the channels open to the Red Cross. This would have been an absurd act for a professional secret service agent, as the Red Cross post was read by both sides' censorship authorities as a regular drill; by a curious freak of fate, this turned out later to her secret advantage. Some records of her name made by the British censorship served to prove that she was genuinely trying to help, when later she got in touch with the British; but we anticipate.[6] Meanwhile she kept her eyes and ears open for reliable safe houses and reliable friends; she read the newspapers carefully, the ones published under German control, to study all the rules about control of movement. From the underground press she took care to keep as clear as she could, having grasped intuitively one of the ground rules of secret activity – never take an unnecessary risk.

There were necessary risks enough. The networks run by Nurse Cavell, the Princesse de Croy and others out of Belgium in 1914–18 had no farther to go than the Dutch border. The Netherlands were now in German occupation as well; so was Luxembourg, as before.

92

The nearest neutral frontier, the Swiss, was much farther away, beyond Alsace (and Alsace was now part of Hitler's Reich), was still more difficult to cross, and led into a military cul-de-sac, for Switzerland was entirely surrounded by Axis or satellite states. Andrée correctly appreciated that Vichy France was not to be relied on. The Belgian coast, though closest to England, was impenetrably heavily guarded for all its forty-two miles' length; even if the guards could be bribed, there were no boats to be had. This left Spain, as the last resort; however unpromising pro-Axis Spain might turn out to be under Franco's dictatorship, there was no other way out. Andrée determined to try it.

This in turn raised a practical problem: money. None of her close relations was rich; her parents had indeed lately had to sell off their own freehold, at 73 avenue Emile Verhaeren in Schaerbeek, and to become the new owner's tenants. Her father knew that she was interesting herself in the fate of British prisoners, and in the general problems of escape; he was too sensible to ply her with questions. She in turn took care not to be too explicit with him about what she was doing, for several reasons. Anyone could see that the fewer people knew what she was up to, the safer it would be for all concerned and besides, she was fond of him. She knew that he would want to join in whatever risks were being run, and preferred to keep him out of danger. Besides, he was already fifty-four, and all the friends whom she first collected as her companions were much younger, her own contemporaries. She was then twenty-five.

What she envisaged was far too complicated to be undertaken single-handed. She brought together to do it people she knew well already, fellow nurses, fellow students, fellow artists. They were all young, all ardent, all anti-Nazi, all good Belgians, and all keen to fight in a non-violent way if they could. And someone put up the indispensable starting sum of money, so that they could begin. Who this anonymous benefactor was has never (so far as I know) been published. Andrée de Jongh knew, and having a sense of honour as keen as her sense of patriotism did not forget; she made sure the debt was cleared eventually.

The group thereupon organized itself for action. Andrée dyed her hair black, and took the simple codename of 'Dedée'. She sent her friend Arnold Deppé off to the Spanish frontier to reconnoitre, where he met a Belgian refugee, Mme Elvire de Greef, who became a vital link in the line as it developed. Mme de Greef – known as 'Tante Go' after a favourite bull-terrier of hers called Go-Go – was a thoroughly capable woman: 'you could see at sight she was a born organizer', according to a Frenchman much skilled in the ways of resistance, no mean organizer himself.[7] Her husband Fernand, speaking good German as well as his native French and Flemish, had a job as interpreter in the German *Kommandantur* at Anglet, between Bayonne and Biarritz, where the de Greefs had rented a villa; this gave him access to blank identity cards, special pass forms and rubber stamps. This access helped to solve one of the line's main problems: how to equip those travelling on it with the papers necessary for passing the routine police controls that were one of the tiresome features of the occupation. The rest were produced by a professional engraver in Belgium.

The de Greefs had got as far as Anglet in the exodus of 1940, had been unable to get farther, and had stayed there; made friends with the mayor; looked after some 900 fellow-countrymen also stranded in the neighbourhood and cast round for some way of doing harm to their conquerors. Hence Monsieur's job at the *Kommandantur*; hence several contacts with the local smugglers; hence a password Madame left with an intelligence circuit friend in Brussels, 'Is it true that poor Go-Go is dead?', by which anyone who wanted to be smuggled across the frontier could be identified to her.

Deppé's contacts in Brussels were extensive enough for him to have heard of this, and he produced the password at the Villa. 'Tante Go' threw herself readily into the enterprise, and Deppé was soon back in Brussels with plentiful assurances that all was going to be well. He and 'Dedée' set off with the first party of passengers, eleven of them. They got across the frontier into France without trouble, but ran into a check on the river Somme, near Corbie above Amiens. There was to have been a boat; it had disappeared. 'Dedée' got hold of a coil of thin rope, swam the Somme, passed the bight of the rope round a stout tree, swam back, and shepherded the whole party across, one by one. She said afterwards that her only worry was what a fool she would look, in dripping underclothes, if a passing sentry noticed and arrested them.[8] A farmhouse near the southern bank welcomed them, and gave them a chance to dry out.

Deppé, who knew the Bayonne area well already, took the party on across France – a comparatively easy matter, since they all spoke fluent French. Long though the route was that Andrée de Jongh had foreseen – over a thousand kilometres from Brussels to Hendaye – it had the countervailing advantage that a lot of it could be covered by train, without any need to cross the demarcation line and produce an *Ausweis* to do so. The whole route was in the occupied zone.

Andrée was not going to let Arnold Deppé take all the risks by himself. She went too, and met for the first time 'Tante Go'; they took to each other instantly. The only difficulty Madame de Greef raised was the virtual impossibility of hiding a party as large as thirteen in a place as gossipy as refugee-filled Bayonne, or in anywhere as mildly countrified as her villa at Anglet, where everyone in the neighbourhood knew everyone else, and strangers were spotted at a glance.

Yet this was just the sort of challenge to which the de Greefs enjoyed rising. With the help of their smuggling friends, the eleven passengers were soon across the Pyrenees where the Spanish police collared the lot. Two eventually got through to England, one man and one woman, four got stuck in Miranda camp, and five, all Belgian officers, were handed back by the Spanish police to the Germans.

Unhappily for the line, one of these said more than an officer should have done about where he had been and whom he had seen. Among other direct results, the Gestapo in Brussels secured a description of Arnold Deppé, and one either of Andrée de Jongh or of another girl Deppé knew – also working in the line – who looked quite like her, and was also called Andrée: Andrée Dumon. Arnold Deppé and Andrée de Jongh, unaware that the thread holding this sword of Damocles above their heads had lost another strand, spent the spring of 1941 organizing their next party, again of eleven: eight Belgians and three British. The night before they were due to leave, two of these three were arrested in Brussels. This left Andrée in charge of two Belgians and a Scotsman – Colin Cupar, who had evaded capture when the Highland Division surrendered at Saint-Valéry-en-Caux in June 1940. He had no French at all. Deppé was to take the six other Belgians by a different route, and join Andrée at Corbie. She got to Corbie; Deppé did not. He and his party, she discovered eventually, had been denounced by a supposed friend of his, and arrested in the train out of Brussels. She had been marked down into it as well, having slipped in in the main station for a last-minute word with him. The nark who saw her enter the train went off to report it, and did not see her leave the train a moment later and go back to her own, more local, train, which took a direction that would save Private Cupar from having to answer questions in French at a large customs post.

She determined to carry on, with her three companions, had no adventures in Paris and caused less stir than before at the de Greefs' villa, as the party was so much smaller. When Madame de Greef asked her how she would feel if, again, her whole party was rounded up in Spain, she had a sublimely simple reply: they would not be rounded up, because she would go into Spain with them to make sure they were not. And she did.

'Tomas', the Basque smuggler in charge of this particular frontier crossing, looked dubious; Andrée de Jongh would not be gainsaid. She had done climbing and walking enough in the Ardennes to take goat-tracks in the western Pyrenees in her stride. 'Tomas' set off at a brisk pace, on foot, took them across the summer shallows of the Bidassoa without a hitch, and then did eight hours' solid up-and-down walking along the hill paths in the dark. She followed his every step, too tough and too proud to ask for a halt. Cupar and the two Belgians came after, too ashamed to ask for a halt when she did not.

'Tomas' left them in a remote farmhouse, where they were devoured by fleas while – and even before – they slept. The farmer was a Basque with no French and only a few words of Spanish, which in turn Andrée hardly spoke. 'Santiago', a local man, took Andrée into San Sebastian, and advised her that if she took the very early train to Bilbao, there would be no police control. She and her three evaders took it and she turned up, Cupar still in tow, at the British consulate.

His presence authenticated her, in the eyes of the vice-consul who saw her (the consul happened to be away). After five minutes with Cupar, he came back and gave her a long interview. He just sat, puffing at a pipe, encouraging her to talk (in French); his manner inspired confidence; she talked. She asked whether she might have Cupar's fare back – 6,000 Belgian francs, plus 1,400 for the guides; not for herself, but so that she could recoup the friend who had lent it to her. She then proposed to deliver as many British troops as she could find in, and move out of, Belgium thus removing the danger from the Belgians who sheltered them, and making the troops available again for the war. Would this interest the British?

Would she care to come back next morning? Certainly. 'Santiago' had recommended her a small hotel, where she could afford to stay; she had a little money left over. (Later she discovered that 'Santiago' had paid for her in advance.) She was patient enough to sit indoors without getting bored; it turned out she needed her patience. She was kept waiting ten days, daily asked to return next day, while the wires were busy between Bilbao, Madrid, Lisbon and London.

In London, both secret service authorities and diplomats had a word to say. MI9, the recently formed escape service, was intensely interested, but had by no means got freedom of action. On anything that MI6 chose to regard as a point of interest to itself, 9 was 6's subordinate and Claude Dansey, to whom Andrée de Jongh's adventure was referred, at once denounced it as a Gestapo plant, what in Russia is called a *provocatsia*. The vice-consul who had actually met Andrée protested that her radiant integrity could not be faked, and slow leave to trust the man on the spot was wrung from Dansey. Andrée was given not only Cupar's fare but her own, and – by arrangement with the Belgian government in exile – those of the two officers she had brought with her also; she was assured of a warm welcome, and further reimbursement, if she cared to call again.

Dansey was wrong to suspect a trap, but right to divine a keen degree of Gestapo interest in what was going on. The German police, tipped off by Deppé's supposed friend, knew that Andrée de Jongh was at work on some anti-German project. While she was on her way back to Brussels, two plain-clothes detectives in belted raincoats called on her father at home. They did not even bother to remove their hats indoors. Where was his younger daughter? In Bruges, he believed. What did he mean, he believed? Ah well, the young nowadays, you know – and it passed off with a snarl and a caution. Frédéric de Jongh found his knees trembling after he had seen them back into the street. He then began working for the line himself; his office desk was soon full of blank identity cards and ration books.[9] (The school still stands in Schaerbeek, in the Place Gaucheret; it is now named after him.) He had no way of communicating, for sure, with Andrée but managed by luck to get a common friend to intercept her while she was still just outside Belgium, at Valenciennes,[10] with a message that the Gestapo were looking for her.

She simply shifted her own base, staying as a rule in Paris herself, between journeys to the Spanish frontier, on the assumption that she would be harder to find in a large town than in any village; collecting parties from Belgium at the Gare du Nord, shepherding them promptly across the city into a train for the south, and taking them on from there. Often girls she had recruited in Belgium would arrive with these parties, and help her with the innumerable minor complications of the Paris Metro and the main line trains.

She made up her own mind what she wanted to do, and which risks she wanted to run; she was responsive also to her fellow-workers' opinions, so far as they could reach her. What both she and all her companions were determined to resist was any sort of outside dictation, whether from Berlin, or from Moscow, or from London (Washington was not yet in the war). Moscow hardly came into it: there is no perceptible trace of Comintern influence on, or indeed interest in, the line at all.

Berlin came into it much too often, through providing the incessant controls through or round which escapers and evaders had to be ferried. (A word of definition: an escaper[11] has been in enemy hands and got away, an evader has never been in enemy hands at all.) Through these controls, and their operations in large towns, on frontiers, and on main line trains, Berlin came to exercise some degree of impact on the line; more and more as time went on. Of the earliest prisoners, as we saw just now, one talked too much. Arnold Deppé kept a proud and sullen silence; not all his companions in misfortune were quite so stoical. Berlin in any case was the enemy's headquarters, to be fought against *à outrance*.

London was both the seat of the Belgian government in exile, and the capital of one of the great powers – from 22 June 1940 to 22 June 1941, the only great power – at war with Berlin; yet Andrée de Jongh and all her friends were determined to call no man master. She met, on her second visit to Bilbao – in mid-October 1941 – the man MI9 called 'Monday': (Sir) Michael Cresswell, then a second secretary at the Madrid embassy in his very early thirties.[12] They got on thoroughly well, but she remained impervious to almost all his suggestions that the British might help in the actual running of the line by sending in a few trained wireless operators and by offering some technical advice. Her and her colleagues' fierce desire for independence made them suspicious of every sort of offer of help that might imply any degree of control, and they thought that to take on a wireless operator would only multiply the risks of detection.

The one point she did take in was the importance to the Allied war effort of rescuing trained aircrew. She went so far as to promise that she would mention this to her friends in Belgium, some of whom took the idea up with enthusiasm. Before long, the line, which Cresswell first called 'Postman' – its name was changed later to the more appropriate 'Comet' – was handling aircrew regularly. By the time, late in 1942, that it could pass back the crew of a heavy bomber shot down over Holland into Spain in a week, it had firmly established its value in the eyes of the British: not only MI9, but MI6, the air ministry, the war cabinet even, were prepared to do all they could to help it.

Help hinged, necessarily, on communications, and these could only be made through Andrée de Jongh, whenever she had occasion to cross into Spain. She usually managed to indicate, through Mme de Greef, when she would be coming, and 'Monday' always made a point of driving over to Bilbao to see her. The welcomes he gave her encouraged her, even if they had to have a long argument in which he failed to persuade her to accept a wireless operator, or to get her father to leave his post of extreme danger in Brussels.

Her unfailing welcome in Bilbao was not the only feature of these journeys that cheered her, besides the feeling of a task accomplished. She had made a new friend in the mountains; the Basque guide who had accompanied her on her first journey northward on foot, back into occupied territory. He hardly ever failed to travel with her thereafter, for the rest of the time she was free.

He was a giant of a man, Florentino Giocoechea; a huge bearlike countryman from Ciboure on the French Biscay coast. He only spoke Basque, and knew the mountains better than he knew the back of his hand. Once on a rough winter night, when an airman evader shrank at the spectacle of the foaming Bidassoa, Florentino simply picked him up and carried him across piggyback. His one weakness was cognac; even that he turned into a strength. He hid bottles of it here and there on the mountains, nosed them out in the dark, and could not very well be refused a swig by his companions when he had found them, and thus shown that he had not lost his way. Andrée and Florentino made an ideal team; his strength and knowledge combined splendidly with her bravery and verve. They seldom had any trouble finding their way, and on the rare occasions when he did go astray, he knew the hill paths – not to speak of the brandy caches – so intimately that he could rapidly get back onto the right track again. She – as they came to fall into a kind of routine, even for so *outré* a way of passing the time – often used to go last in each party, to cheer on anybody inclined to straggle. No man, in that even more man-dominated society than the present, could bear the thought that a slip of a girl was prepared to press on through danger, darkness and the unknown, while he was going to hang back. 'One man told me', wrote Neave, whose job it became to interrogate the people who travelled down this line when they got to London, 'that he was only able to continue by watching Dedée's slim legs in front of him in the dawn light.'[13]

Neave several times found that the men he was talking to had tears in their eyes when they spoke of Dedée. This can be dismissed as sentimentalism; all the same, there was something more than a little moving, for those who had themselves reached safety, in the spectacle of this slender, attractive girl who had escaped with them, returning of her own free will into the pit from which she had dragged them.

Neave's account of how they usually managed the actual frontier crossing, at the Bidassoa, is worth quoting at some length:

On a clear night, the frontier guards could be seen patrolling the Spanish road. They would not hesitate to fire if they saw anything moving.

Florentino would then give a signal to Dedée, who quietly ordered everyone to remove their trousers and tie them in a bundle round their necks. Florentino climbed down first, to test the depth. If the river was fordable, he would take the first airman by the hand and lead him across with the water up to his waist. It was essential for the party to cling together. One false slip would mean drowning. Dedée would come last, often helping the airmen over herself. Her strength and vitality amazed them.

Shivering from the icy water, they put on their trousers and waited. The sternest test was yet to come. They must climb a rocky embankment, cross the railway line and then the frontier road, followed by a steep slope on the far side. Florentino would lie flat, hidden by a thorn bush, watching the road. He could see lights from the windows of the frontier post [there was of course no blackout in Spain] and a guard patrolling only a hundred yards away. When the guard turned his back, Florentino gave a grunt, clambered over the railway, jumped to the road and scrambled up the opposite slope. Pulling himself upwards with the help of roots and bushes, his great strength enabled him to get clear and out of sight in a few seconds. The tired airmen followed him. Sometimes one would fall back into the road with a clatter. Dedée would always wait to see that every man was safely across and sometimes would seize one and push him up the bank. How could the men fail before this extraordinary girl? By sheer force of example, she drove them on into Spain.[14]

Once in Spain, there was a hard damp night's walk ahead, and thunderous rain often made it damper. Dedée, on her very first northward crossing of the Pyrenees, had encountered a tempest so severe that she and Florentino fell repeatedly on the slippery paths; he was tipsier than usual, and had insisted each time on a kiss before he would stand up. Hence her rule that he was at least to start out sober; and hence her comparative calm when the sky again burst round her. Some of the airmen who could face, stolidly enough, their contemporary dangers on active service – moving fast through the air in aluminium tubes, surrounded by lethal quantities of fuel and explosive – found it easy to flinch in the face of much older perils, of torrent, storm and mountain. Dedée's assumption that these perils were as normal and as surmountable as a shower of rain in a city street carried them along with her into safety.

She and Florentino brought out fifty-four people, most of them aircrew, in the four months of July to October 1942 alone. She herself made thirty-two double trips through the mountains in all, convoying 110 people;[15] but already by the summer of 1942 she could feel the breath of the Gestapo getting hot on the back of her neck. The Schaerbeek house had been raided again, in February. Her father had the good luck to be out, but her sister Suzanne Wittek was arrested, and succumbed, long after the war, to the treatment she had received in a concentration camp. Her arrest only made her father more angrily determined to work on for 'Comet' but Dedée now joined her own entreaties to MI9's, and at last he agreed. On 30 April he left Brussels for Paris, leaving his step-grandchildren in charge of his wife. They never saw him again. He kept changing cover names and moving house; it was as well that he did. Within ten days of his flight, several of his friends in Brussels were arrested and it looked, from MI9's angle of sight, as if 'Comet' would be seen no more in the wartime sky.

MI9 underestimated both the resilience and the courage of the de Jonghs, and indeed of most of the Belgians. Frédéric de Jongh had been in touch, in complete secrecy, with Baron Jean Greindl (called 'Nemo' when the line got to know him better), who was director of

102

a small Red Cross organization that provided food, sent in from Sweden, for deserving cases: children, in particular. Greindl had stretched a point, without consulting the Swedish diplomats with whom he dealt – thus safeguarding their neutrality. He had constantly provided the headmaster with food enough to keep half a dozen men alive. He was able, discreetly and unobtrusively as always, to pick up the threads of the line when de Jongh had had to let them drop. He organized its affairs, on a less centralized – and therefore safer – basis, so that a delicate, widespread net of sure friends covered all Belgium.

The Germans continued to press the line, so far as it was perceptible to them, as hard as they could. For instance, they arrested that summer the nineteen-year-old Andrée Dumon ('Nadine') – for whom Andrée de Jongh may have been mistaken in the circuit's early days – after she had made one escorting journey to Paris too many, and had been noticed after getting twenty men away. Her younger sister Micheline ('Michou') took over her work, and more than doubled her score – she moved forty-four aircrew from Belgium to Paris in the course of 1943.

But 1943 was a gloomy year for 'Comet', and for the de Jonghs.

In January, Andrée at last persuaded her father – then sharing a flat with her in the rue Vaneau, near the Invalides – that it really had become too dangerous for him to stay in Paris, and late on the 13th they both left by train for Bayonne, with three young pilots. Next day they presented themselves to Mme de Greef at her Anglet villa, in the middle of a storm of tremendous proportions, that had made the Bidassoa quite unfordable.

Florentino, undismayed, proposed to take the pilots on an extra detour, by a bridge farther up the river that he reckoned would be unguarded on a foul night. But this meant an extra five hours' marching, for which Frédéric de Jongh, close on sixty, was palpably unfit. Andrée and 'Tante Go' persuaded him to stay at Anglet, while Andrée and the pilots set off towards the Pyrenees, stopping for an evening meal on the first night, as had become her custom, at a farm above Urrugne, just off the main road to Hendaye.

She had never known the rain so violent, or the paths so foul;

Florentino agreed with her there could be no thought of crossing that night. He went off to his home and his wife in Ciboure, a few miles to the north-east.

Neither he nor Andrée was much perturbed by a chance call, while the whole party were drying off in front of the farmhouse fire, by a Spanish labourer whom Andrée had once employed as a guide, and dismissed for suspected pilfering. At noon next day a party of armed Germans arrived, arrested everybody at the farm, and searched it from attic to cellar for 'the missing man': they had presumably been tipped off by the chance caller, who needed money. (He vanished, and was never tracked down.[16]) One of the pilots talked.

The house that had sheltered him for a few hours in Bayonne was raided – it belonged to one of 'Tante Go's' best helpers, Jean Dassié, who had lost an arm in the previous war. He, his wife and his daughter were packed off to Germany, where they were treated so harshly that he died a few days, and his wife a few months, after they were freed.

Andrée was not at first the object of much German suspicion. The de Greefs and their friend Jean-François Nothomb ('Franco') made repeated attempts to spring her from prison, but none of them worked quite fast enough. She was taken away to prison in Paris before they could get her out of the local jail. Altogether she underwent nineteen interrogations by Luftwaffe intelligence, besides two by the Gestapo, the much more alarming secret state police. Luckily for her, the two bodies were in rivalry with each other and the Luftwaffe people maintained an interest in her as long as they could, to keep her out of the clutches of the Gestapo. It was useless for her to pretend innocence: she had been caught in the company of three RAF evaders. But neither the Luftwaffe, nor the Gestapo, believed the one true statement she made, that it was she who was in charge of the entire escape line. Her interrogators could not credit an operation of this size and complexity to someone so young, such an *ingénue* in appearance and manner, and not even – as they all were – a man.

She claimed control of 'Comet' for two reasons: first because it was true, and also because she wanted to do all she could to shield all her friends in it, above all her father. He had gone back to the rue Vaneau, and under the cover name of Moreau was working harder than ever, to avenge his daughters' arrests. He continued to meet parties from Brussels at the Gare du Nord, hide them if necessary in Paris, improve their papers if need be, and send them off to the south-west.

Three weeks after Andrée's arrest, the Brussels Gestapo – acting quite independently of their colleagues in France – mounted a major attack on 'Comet', and captured Jean Greindl, the working organizer. He spent seven months in close, usually solitary, confinement, and by a stroke of irony was killed by an Allied bomb in an air raid on 7 September 1943. An SOE agent who had changed sides, and was doing his best to help the enemy, in the next cell to him, was killed by the same bomb.[17] Seven of his friends and colleagues were shot on 20 October at the Tir National, the Brussels shooting range where Edith Cavell had been executed in 1915.

Frédéric de Jongh did not survive them. A traitor had by now been infiltrated into the line, and led the Germans to him on 7 June 1943. He was arrested, with two companions, on the platform of the Gare du Nord as he shook hands with a party of six airmen – five English and one American – who arrived from Brussels accompanied by the traitor, Desoubrie, as their guide. {Desoubrie was caught eventually and executed after the war.)

There could be no doubt of his guilt. He was held for some time in Fresnes prison; his interrogators got nothing from him. He was allowed to write occasional letters to his wife. In the last of these, he said: 'Dedée mustn't reproach herself. If I hadn't done what I have done with her, I would have done it with other people.'[18] His own fate, as he knew by then, was sealed. They sent him to Mont Valérien.

This mid-nineteenth century fort dominates a bend of the Seine in the western suburbs of Paris. Napoleon III used to live in the palace of Saint-Cloud near by, which was burned down during the Commune. Nearly five thousand resisters were sent there during the Nazi occupation of France; not one came back alive.

There is a little space, deep inside the fort, about half the size of a lawn-tennis court, where all in turn were taken, by ones and twos or in small parties, to be shot by the Wehrmacht. Next to a corner of Katyn forest, it is the dreariest spot in Europe; without the horror of the killing-sites of the death camps in Poland, or the sombre grandeur of the chapel in the Tower or of the Bridge of Sighs, an air of helplessness still lies heavy on it. The parade ground outside bears a huge Cross of Lorraine in its cobbles, and twice a year all the principal surviving heroes and heroines of Gaullist resistance assemble for a service of homage and recollection; on 18 June, the anniversary of de Gaulle's original appeal (the day after Jean Moulin tried to kill himself), and on 11 November, the anniversary of the armistice of 1918. There are sixteen tombs in the thickness of the fort's wall; fifteen of them holding the remains of different kinds of Free French or resistance fighter – a merchant seaman, a clandestine courier, and so on. In the sixteenth tomb, the last surviving Companion of Resistance is to be laid; the Companions, fewer each time, cannot help eyeing each other a shade morbidly when they parade. Not many of them recall Frédéric de Jongh, who was not even a Frenchman; he was nevertheless as gallant a resister as any of them, and father of another.

'Comet' survived even these runs of arrests. The d'Oultremont brothers, aristocrats, took over the Belgian end from 'Nemo'; one of them was drowned in the Bidassoa in December 1943; the line stayed in being. Nothomb, 'Franco', took over Andrée de Jongh's role as courier and organizer in France until his own arrest in January 1944, again at the hands of Desoubrie. The line was inextinguishable; her friends made sure of that. 'Michou' and Peggy van Lier, both in their teens, kept it going, till they in turn were persuaded to come out along it;[19] it was still at work after the Normandy landings in June. Such was the strength of Andrée's companionship.

The rest of her own wartime story can soon be told. She was taken to Brussels, where she managed to have a few words with Jean Greindl in a police waiting-room; they could do no more than keep up each others' spirits. It slowly dawned on the Luftwaffe staff who tried to pump her for information that they were not going to get

106

any from her, so they released her back to the Gestapo. She came within the reach of the notorious *Nacht und Nebel* order; those who opposed too actively the Nazis' new arrangements, and were caught, were to disappear into the night and fog of the concentration camp system. She was sent to Ravensbrück, and any inquiries launched about her fate, by her family or her friends or anyone else, were met with total silence. Efforts were made by neutral diplomats, egged on from high quarters in London, to arrange her exchange for practically anybody (except Hess) the Nazis cared to name; no reply at all. By this time Himmler, who controlled the camps, was much more powerful in Nazi Germany than Ribbentrop, the foreign minister, through whom diplomats dealt; Himmler's men said nothing.

Ravensbrück is a small town in the Prussian plain, fifty miles north of Berlin. A concentration camp for women was set up there in May 1939, and during the war was busy. Conditions there were grim, beyond the belief of those who have never experienced captivity, far grimmer even than in prisoner of war camps or in most civil prisons. We shall have quite enough grimness in the following chapter, when we have to deal with Auschwitz; her sufferings can be guessed at. She had the good sense and good fortune to disappear quietly into the crowds of women, known only by numbers; even the Gestapo lost sight of her. She knew that she had done what she should; she had nothing with which she needed to reproach herself. She used her nurse's training to alleviate her fellow prisoners' lot a trifle and waited for the war to end.

When it was over, she went quietly back to Schaerbeck to look after her mother. Not for her the torments of publicity that attend the life of a national heroine; she kept herself quietly to herself.

As soon as she had recovered physically from her two years on a diet of turnip soup, and was sure that her nephew and nieces and her mother did not need her any more, she remembered Father Damien, that other heroic figure of her childhood. She went to work in a leper colony in the Belgian Congo; survived the troubles of 1960 and moved on to another at Addis Ababa. When her mother died, the RAF happened to run a training flight from Addis to Brussels, on which she could travel free, and ran her back to Addis after she had cleared up the estate.

Eventually she allowed herself a little rest, and has come back to Belgium to live out whatever years remain. The King of the Belgians has raised her to the rank of countess; she still keeps herself to herself.

7

Witold Pilecki

The 'Comet' line was kept alive by people in their twenties and by teenagers. Andrée de Jongh survived partly because she was uncommonly tough, and partly because she had such an ingenuous air, that appealed to the sentimentalism of her captors. In eastern Europe there was no room for sentiment. We must now move off the slopes of the western Pyrenees on to the full rigours of the frozen east European plain, and a war without mercy.

The horrors of the eastern front have never been altogether appreciated in the kinder world of the west. The English, having had no foreign invasion for over three centuries and no foreign conquest for over nine, have already forgotten what the Nazis had set down in their plan after they had won the Battle of Britain. It began with taking all able-bodied men between the ages of seventeen and forty-five away to labour camps in central or eastern Europe. Later, blondes between eighteen and twenty-five were to enter stud farms to produce good Aryan stock. Not many English people are sorry the Battle of Britain went the other way.

In the east, in Poland and later in Russia, the Nazis were briefly able to experiment on a lavish scale to suit every whim of their racist fantasies, and those whims were many. To a devout Nazi SS stormtrooper, the non-Aryan peoples who lived in conquered eastern territories were not proper men and women and children, with the same rights as Aryan human beings: they were a sort of biped cattle. An SS-man would shoot a Jew with as little compunction as a farmer shoots a rabbit; some SS-men were as quick on the trigger with

communists, or even Poles or Russians of no proved political lean-
ings, as they were with Jews.

Even before the war, Hitler, Goering and Himmler had privately
decided what they were going to do to the Jews – wipe them out.
The eastern conquests provided an opportunity to make a start, at
least. Poland had a Jewish population of several million, readily
identifiable, as they had kept themselves to themselves for centuries
– partly by their own choice, partly because a great many Poles were
almost as anti-semitic as the Nazis. For example, in 1938 hardly any
officers in the Polish armed forces were Jews, and none of the few
that were, were young.[1] A few Jewish banking families, and a very
few families of the Jewish intelligentsia, had joined the Polish
landowning ruling class, mainly by marriage.[2] The great bulk of the
Polish Jews still lived in ghettoes, as they had done since the seven-
teenth century, and were fiercely confined to them, for the time
being, by the Nazis in western Poland. Fifteen special groups of SS
toured the countryside, rounding up fugitives for the ghettoes, unless
they found it more convenient to massacre them, and anyone who
sheltered them, on the spot.

Eastern Poland was under Soviet Russian occupation from mid-
September 1939 till it was overrun by the Germans in the summer
of 1941 when the SS special groups moved eastwards, and worked
harder. It also included a substantial Jewish population, as did such
large Ukrainian cities as Kiev and Kharkov, which fell into German
hands a few weeks later. The USSR was notorious for anti-semitism
in the 1970s, but was much more mildly so than the Nazis had been
and in wartime was hardly anti-semitic at all. At least 300,000 Polish
Jews fled into the Soviet zone of Poland in the autumn of 1939,
before the Soviet authorities shut the border in November. Most of
them were shunted on to Siberia, in no gentle manner, but at least
they were not marked down for death, as the Jews in German-
occupied Poland were.[3]

By this time, Himmler was matching up opportunity and means.
In the spring of 1940 he had picked on Auschwitz, 'an unhealthy,
malaria-ridden, poorly industrialized, ugly town' of some 12,000
people, west of Cracow,[4] as a suitable site for what he meant to do.

He took over an old Austro-Hungarian artillery barracks, of some twenty decrepit and filthy brick huts, and round them caused to be built an extermination camp of which the memory will live long.

The Auschwitz group of camps, including the vast parallel blocks of huts at Birkenau, which covered a site larger than London's Hyde Park a couple of miles from Auschwitz town, has a unique position in human infamy. Nowhere else on earth is there an area of only fifteen square miles, in which in less than five years, nearer four than three million people have been put to death.

Politically, the area lay at the southernmost tip of the large slice of Poland annexed by Germany in 1939, and incorporated into the Third Reich. In principle, the Polish peasantry in all this territory was to be dispossessed, moved away eastward into the rump of Poland, the satellite state called the General Government which the Germans ruled from Warsaw, and replaced by sound Aryans. There were a few coal mines near by: coal mining was dirty work, Poles could carry on with that – under German direction of course. All this shifting of population took time to plan and to arrange. Meanwhile, there were Poles all round Auschwitz, who could not fail to be aware that a huge hutted camp was being built under SS supervision.

Word got round Poland quite fast. The Poles still thought of Poland as one, though their pre-war republic had been partitioned out of existence: the government was in exile, successively in Bucarest, Paris, Bordeaux and London. Most of the north and west of the country was included in the Reich, a strip in the north-east in Lithuania, for nine months, till in June 1940 Lithuania was annexed by the USSR, as all eastern Poland had been in September 1939 and, for what it was worth, the General Government, a subordinate corner of the Reich.

Even before the brief, disastrous campaign of September 1939, the Poles had given some thought to how they might resist a successful invader. Gubbins, the Scot who was later the mainspring of SOE during the world war, journeyed secretly that summer to Poland and the Baltic states, and suggested some useful points to people in authority.[5] The Poles already had long traditions of resistance, for all through the nineteenth century they had been struggling against

111

Habsburg, Hohenzollern and Romanov occupation at once; none of the three as bad as the Nazis, but none of them Polish . All Poles knew, from the cradle, from their parents' and their grandparents' knees, something of what occupation had been and would be like; they all knew the elementary duties of secrecy and silence, the duties the French found it so expensive to learn.

Nazi rule was sterner and fiercer than they had anticipated, but they all rose to its challenge; practically to a man. Poland was alone among the countries the Germans occupied in having no classes of collaborators, people who were ready to work with the enemy, lining their own pockets while they did so.[6] It had clandestine newspapers, almost immediately; several unusually efficient escape lines, running through Hungary and Romania to Turkey; clandestine intelligence traffic with the government in exile, busy all through the war, and almost too many private and secret armies.[7]

Eventually these secret armies were reduced to three: the *Armia Krajowa*, the Home Army of the government in exile[8], the *Armia Ludowa* or People's Army of the pro-communist puppet government set up at Lublin in July 1944 and the *Narodwe Sile Zbrojne* or National Armed Forces, a small extreme right-wing body of practically fascist inclination. Even the NSZ would not cooperate with the Nazis, because they were foreigners. As Count Raczynski, the foreign minister of the Polish government in London, once put it, 'Poland had no Quisling and no Pétain.'[9]

There were plenty of potential leaders about, in the earliest stages, as Poland hummed like an overturned beehive and the Poles tried to recover from the double disruption of their almost simultaneous defeat, from the west and from the east. For a patriotic Pole, the war was not simply a two-sided one of us against them: both Germans and Russians were enemies, even after 22 June 1941, when they started fighting each other.

The Russians, quicker on the draw in this respect than the Germans, determined to cleanse their zone of its leadership classes promptly. They had moved away eastwards by Christmas 1939 over a million people: everyone they could catch who belonged to the well-educated classes – officers, priests, doctors, engineers, advocates, professors, schoolteachers. Four thousand two hundred and fifty-four of the officers were found in 1943, each with his hands bound behind him, each with a bullet through the back of his neck, packed into mass graves in the forest of Katyn. Ten thousand more officers vanished altogether, for over half a century; *Glasnost* in the end revealed the truth. In 1990 even Moscow admitted that the NKVD had shot them all.[10] The Gestapo, less prompt than the NKVD in 1939, let it be known that the 20,000 officers in German-occupied Poland were to report to internment camps; 400 answered the call.

It is with one of the 19,600 who did not answer the call that this chapter deals; a cavalry subaltern in the 13th Uhlans, Polish lancers, called Witold Pilecki. There have been more famous cavalry subalterns in history. The great William Pitt, later first Earl of Chatham, was originally heard of, in Walpole's phrase, as a 'terrible cornet of horse'; Winston Churchill saw service as a subaltern in the Fourth Hussars before ever he turned to politics. These heroes worked on a far grander scale, building and destroying empires; the epic quality in their work could be matched, on a narrower and crueller stage, by this unassertive Pole.

Pilecki, though still only a junior officer in his middle forties, was someone of enormous force of character, even in a society that teemed with people of strong character and intense individuality. He belonged to a body called the *Tajna Armia Polska*, the Secret Polish Army; a body that merged eventually into the AK, the Home Army. It would be misleading to say he played a prominent part in the TAP, because as every Pole knew it was indispensable not to be prominent, for anyone working clandestinely against an occupier; but he was extremely active. Several much more senior people knew and trusted him, and he was aware of a great deal that was going on.

Reports of the camp under construction at Oświęcim – the Polish name for Auschwitz – reached and impressed him, and he conceived a daring plan to do something about it. The plan was so daring that for several weeks his colonel hesitated to approve. It was simply – most daring plans are simple – to let himself get arrested, and sent to Auschwitz as a prisoner. Having got there, he was to send out reports of what was really happening inside the camp, to see whether he could organize resistance, and then, if he could, to escape.

On top of the military difficulties of these tasks, the personal ones were severe. He had married a dozen years earlier, and had a daughter, but Poland's crisis was such that merely personal troubles just had to be brushed aside. Mobilization overrode the marriage tie; his heart could and did stay with his wife and child, but his body had to go elsewhere.

A little time had to be spent on arranging the essential details about communications: a very few addresses, reckoned perfectly safe, which he had to memorize, and a safe, simple password system by which a messenger could establish good faith, were all that were needed. The TAP was a brisk and efficient body, though its leaders were already on the run from the Gestapo. It could clear up swiftly business of this sort, over which café-conversationalist resisters in Bucarest or Paris could dally for months, even years.

And by a stroke of luck, Pilecki secured a false identity which, he reckoned, ought to earn him a sentence to Auschwitz, his first objective: the identity of Tomasz Serafiński, a reserve officer who had gone underground instead of reporting to the Germans as ordered. Pilecki did not know – he did not need to know – where Serafiński had gone. He found out instead enough about Serafiński's past to survive cross-questioning in his new character and he knew that the German secret police, as methodical as they were cruel, had secured a list of all the peacetime officers in the Polish army, active and reserve. To be on this list, and (like the other 19,599) not to have surrendered oneself, would – he reckoned – be crime enough to merit consignment to Auschwitz.

His reckoning proved correct.

It was not difficult to get arrested. He just failed to run away down the nearest side street, one early morning in September 1940 when the Germans made a routine rush-hour check on people walking into central Warsaw to work. He shortly found himself, with a thousand companions, lying face down on the damp sawdust-strewn floor of a nearby riding school. Their hands were stretched out in front of them, palms down. Machine guns covered them from the galleries.

SS men walked among them, whipping those who fidgeted. Pilecki did not fidget.

Two days later, he was received (as Serafiński) in Auschwitz, where he became prisoner number 4,859. In his own words, as he and his companions were marched from the railway station to the camp, 'On the way one of us was ordered to run to a post a little off the road and immediately after him went a round from a machine gun. He was killed. Ten of his casual comrades were pulled out of the ranks and shot on the march with pistols on the ground of "collective responsibility" for the "escape", arranged by the SS-men themselves. The eleven were dragged along by straps tied to one leg. The dogs were teased with the bloody corpses and set onto them. All this to the accompaniment of laughter and jokes.'[11]

They reached the camp as glum, they thought, as could be; marched in under the slogan *Arbeit macht frei*, work sets you free; and were then made glummer still by being made to strip, and to have *all* their hair, body hair as well as face and head hair, shaved off, and to put on the prison uniform of blue-and-white striped canvas and clogs.

Pilecki was lucky enough to get an indoor job, as one of the cleaning staff for his hut, but lost it before long, as the German criminal in charge of the hut would only keep on his staff those who, like himself, habitually clubbed their fellow-prisoners before speaking to them. Not only did he lose his soft job, as well as many other illusions, promptly, he soon almost lost his health, which in such a camp amounted to losing one's life.

On 28 October 1940 a man ran away from an outside working party, and was found to be missing at the noon roll-call. All the prisoners were kept standing at attention on the parade ground from noon till nine in the evening, in an icy north-east wind that bore heavy rain and sleet, turn and turn about. Anyone who moved was liable to be shot. Two hundred died of exposure where they stood. Pilecki was among several hundred more who collapsed, but was nursed back to a semblance of health in the camp hospital, and rapidly returned to work.

The work consisted of building more huts to hold the increased numbers of prisoners who were expected, to store the belongings they brought with them, and in the end to dispose of them and their bodies.

All Nazi concentration camps were run by the SS. Most existed for two reasons – as prisons to sequester those the SS wanted out of the way, and as factories to provide the SS with profits. For this peculiar organization, originally Hitler's small personal bodyguard,[12] grew to be a state-within-a-state of an unusually intricate kind, financing itself in part from the products of its slave labour and with its own private army, the *Waffen-SS*. Through this army's ranks a million men passed; it provided the hard core of Germany's armed forces, nearly forty divisions strong, and included many crack units.[13] Some of its weapons and equipment were, for economy's sake, turned out by the camps that were under SS control.

At and near Auschwitz there were a few arms and chemical factories, but the Auschwitz-Birkenau group of camps existed for a third reason also, more secret and more sinister. Here among other places, here above all, the SS proposed to get on with the *Endlösung*, the final solution of the Jewish problem: the killing of all the Jews they could catch. As Himmler put it to Rudolf Hoess, the founder-commandant of Auschwitz, in the late summer of 1941, 'The Jews are the sworn enemies of the German people and must be eradicated. Every Jew that we can lay our hands on is to be destroyed now during the war, without exception.'[14]

The method chosen was by cyanide gas poisoning. At Auschwitz and Birkenau, as at other extermination camps such as Treblinka, Maidanek, Sobibor, windowless concrete huts were built, with nozzles in their ceilings, into which Jews – or any other prisoners of whom the SS wanted to dispose – were herded, naked, in large crowds, believing they were to have a shower. They were showered with cyanide gas, their bodies were then hauled out and shovelled across to the building next door, also prisoner-built, where they were cremated. On the way from gas chamber to crematorium, the bodies were checked for gold teeth or for rings, which were removed (it was simplest to remove ringed fingers with a garden chopper), to keep the SS profits up.

116

It took time, again, for a scheme of this size and this elaboration to get moving. Auschwitz was founded in 1940; the big killings did not start there till 1942; in January 1945 it was overrun by the Red Army. One thousand two hundred prisoners were left in it at that moment, all too ill to move; in Birkenau there were about 5,800 more invalids, two-thirds of them women.[15] Something approaching four million people had been killed in the complex meanwhile, during the 1,688 days of Auschwitz camp's existence.

During Pilecki's first three months in the camp, nearly 3,000 more prisoners joined it; they were only the beginners. By the summer of 1944 the Auschwitz-Birkenau group of camps had about 130,000 current inmates, sometimes 140,000; but the rate of turnover was very high. For instance, during that summer 437,000 Hungarian Jews were admitted to the camps, almost all of whom were killed when, or soon after, they arrived. In such cases people would be sent straight from the train to the gas chambers, pausing only on the way to undress – several large huts were filled, quite full, with their clothing. They were spared the body-shave Pilecki had gone through; their head hair was shorn after death, on their way to be cremated, and made into mattresses, to keep the SS profits up.

Nearly a thousand prisoners were employed in the *Sonder-kommandos*, the special squads that ran the actual processes of extermination. All were Jews; they were housed, in the end, in the crematorium attics. Each squad worked a twelve-hour shift, turn and turn about with its alternate; about once a quarter, each squad was itself led into the gas chambers by its successor. 'The members of the *Sonder-Kommando*,' as Garliński put it, 'speaking many languages and dialects, could quieten down those being driven to their death, and this they did in the knowledge that they would gain nothing by behaving differently and that by kindly treatment they could at least mitigate the anguish of the victims' last moments.'[16] The death squads themselves knew only too well what awaited them.

All this apparatus of terror was under the guard of about 3,250 SS men.[17] They never moved unarmed, seldom moved singly, and had all the usual adjuncts of a terror camp: tracker dogs, lighted electrified fences, torture chambers, above all, atmosphere. As

Pilecki's example showed us, from the moment they came under SS guard, prisoners were aware that their captors were entirely ruthless. The inmates were encouraged to believe that, as the crematorium squads mostly came to do, they should accept their fate as stoically as they could. They were there to die; they might as well die in a calm and orderly way.

Yet, diabolical as their captors were, they were not diabolically efficient. And in the early months of the camp, they even now and then let people out; it was still just possible to persuade even a member of the Gestapo that he might have made a mistake.

As early as November 1940, two months after his arrest, Pilecki was able to send his first report out of Auschwitz to Warsaw. It was memorized by one of his earliest recruits, a perfectly innocent and inoffensive citizen who had friends in Warsaw powerful enough to persuade the Germans that he had in fact been arrested in error. He was made to swear the customary oaths that he would reveal nothing about what went on inside the camp, but was a good enough Pole and a good enough Catholic to know that oaths sworn under duress have no value. When he made touch with Pilecki's superiors, he talked.

There was not yet much to say. At this date the gas chambers, and the whole Birkenau camp, were no more than gleams in Himmler's and Eichmann's eyes. But at least Home Army headquarters now knew that Auschwitz was a concentration camp, and a cruel one (there were no mild ones) and that Witold Pilecki was at work inside it, seeing what he could do about resistance.

What could he do? First of all, continue to report, for which he seized every opportunity, however glancing, that appeared safe. Some of the SS garrison's laundry, for example, was done for them in Auschwitz town. The SS did not want to demean themselves by carrying laundry baskets; they contented themselves with searching the baskets very thoroughly (such baskets forming a well known means of escape), and providing a vigilant armed guard for the prisoners who toted them. Over the months, their vigilance relaxed a trifle. The camp laundry squad had meanwhile had a chance to assess the characters of the few town laundry workers whom they saw, and, given luck and daring, could slip written notes to them. Any Pole could be relied on to be anti-German, so the notes got passed on to any address they bore.

Any such system bore risks of interception, at any and every stage; people who will not run risks cannot hope to win battles. In 1942–4 a considerable body of intelligence about what was going on inside the camps got passed out of Auschwitz and Birkenau, reached Warsaw safely, and was passed on thence to Stockholm, whence it reached London from March 1941. The London Poles passed the news on to MI6, which passed it to the Foreign Office; thence it went to Washington, Moscow, and any service department that needed it. Some of it the Poles used straight away in their propaganda.

The trouble was that the news was, on the whole, too bad to be credible and most people who heard it, did not take it in as true. Moscow was disinclined to believe anything that emanated from the London Poles, in principle. In Washington and London, everyone in authority, however bellicose towards Nazism, had been brought up to believe mass murder to be utterly beyond the pale of civilized behaviour, and imagined Germany still to be a civilized state. The sheer incredulity of distant senior men lay, unknown to Pilecki, as one obstacle in his path.

Much closer obstacles were only too obvious. The main starting task was to do anything he could to encourage his fellow prisoners not to kowtow, any more than they had to, to the terrorist regime under which they had to live. As most of his fellow prisoners were Poles, this task was not insuperably difficult. In carrying it through, he was able to gauge something of his companions' characters, and to estimate which could be most useful for more advanced work.

He had had to abandon most of his preconceived ideas about what he would do, as soon as he discovered how hard conditions in the camp really were: a process of adapting idea to reality, painful enough in one's teens, that can be excruciating in manhood, especially on the morrow of a great national disaster. He wanted to set up a secret grouping among the prisoners that would be ready to try to wrest power from the SS, the moment there was a nearby

Allied armed force to help. He did take in that there was no probability, no outside likelihood even, that the prisoners could seize
power all by themselves: the SS had too many machine guns, and
were too quick to use them. He hoped for a Russian or an Anglo-
American parachute landing in force or failing that, for a coup by
Polish partisans.

There were in fact some Home Army partisan groups in the
neighbourhood, now and again, though they were neither strong in
numbers nor heavily armed. The Home Army's weakness in arms,
compared to similar groups in France or Greece or Yugoslavia, arose
from two causes: Poland lay at the extreme limit of air range from
Anglo-American territory, and the Russians forbade aircraft on
supply sorties for the Home Army to land on Soviet airfields. The
few aircraft that could manage the round trip – even from Brindisi,
when it became available late in 1943, it was a ten-hour flight –
therefore had to take up most of their load with fuel, to get there and
back. France and Yugoslavia both got about 10,000 tons of warlike
stores by air, through links with SOE and its American opposite
number, OSS (the Office of Strategic Services); Poland only got 600
tons.

The People's Army does not seem to have operated in the parts of
Poland annexed to the Reich. The official Soviet attitude to the
Germans' camps was in any case, to a western eye, slightly odd.
Theoretically – in Marxist-Stalinist theory, that is – no prisoners
were ever taken from the Red Army; a Red Army man's duty was to
fight, never to surrender. The Germans and their satellites took over
six million uniformed prisoners all the same (four-fifths of whom,
by the by, succumbed in German hands – another huge item for the
butcher's bill). Every single survivor who was returned – usually
forcibly, by the other Allies – to the USSR after the war automatically
did a punishment spell in a Siberian labour camp.[18] All camps, of
whatever kind, were looked at askance by the Russians; except for
their own, and their own were inadmissible.

But we must get back from these strategic and political generalities
to the hard particular facts of Pilecki's Auschwitz career. By

Christmas 1940 he had already chosen his first five clandestine leaders; he added two more groups of five in the following spring. An attack of pneumonia, brought on by standing naked on parade for some hours in February while his hut and clothes were disinfested of lice, put him for a month into the camp hospital, where he organized a highly efficient cell. It was (as Peulevé later found in Buchenwald) a part of the camp well adapted for resistance and deception, and the Auschwitz hospital secured, by devious means, a wireless receiver: this freed prisoners in the know from dependence on Goebbels's propaganda bulletins, which were all that the camp loudspeakers ever provided in the way of news. Of course there were no newspapers within the camp.[19]

Attempts to organize resistance were not of course confined to Pilecki and his groups. Several senior Polish officers set about organizing intelligence networks, with varying degrees of success. Unhappily, some among them – some even of the senior officers who became involved in Pilecki's own groupings – occasionally found they had to stand on their dignity, and insisted on receiving orders only from men senior to themselves.[19] Such petty resentments, pathetically out of place in an SS camp, were ineradicable in the old Polish officer caste.

There were differences between Polish prisoners on more important matters than rank: they did not all see eye to eye in politics. Differences in political viewpoint grew more widespread, as the racial composition of the camp's inmates changed. At first the prisoners were nearly all Poles, with a sprinkling of senior Germans, but over thirty nationalities were represented eventually; particularly Russians and Ukrainians, as well as hordes of Jews from several different states. Pilecki preferred dealing with Poles, as communication was so much easier through a common language and common customs, but by no means imposed any sort of racial bar. In any case, while he was in the camp it remained very largely Polish in its prisoner population.

The Communists among the prisoners at first lay low; after 22 June 1941 they hurled themselves into the resistance struggle, not with any outstanding effect. The German Communists in

121

Buchenwald and other camps often held dominant positions; the Polish Communists, starting later in the struggle, were not as a rule as successful. One subsequently well-known politician, Jozef Cyrankiewicz, already – though ten years younger than Pilecki – an eminent Socialist, took a leading part in the politico-military fusion that Pilecki's tact and ability and common sense had created by the time Cyrankiewicz reached the camp in the autumn of 1942. He later drew apart from the right-wing elements whom Pilecki had persuaded to cooperate with the Socialists, threw in his lot with the left-wingers and became prime minister of the new Communist-dominated Poland after the war.

Such actual military organization as Pilecki was able to set up was necessarily slender and tentative and conditions, as well as people, in the camp changed so fast that he found he had to set up different groups to cope with different contingencies. By night, with the prisoners locked in their huge huts, a different set of fighting men would be needed from the grouping that would apply during the day, when prisoners were scattered at work, some inside the camp and some outside it.

A good deal of intricate, deadly secret planning was done on these necessarily conjectural lines, everyone in the early stages taking the usual care to bring nobody else into the plot who was not wholly to be trusted. The one vital necessity was armament which was, at first glance, unavailable.

Reflection showed some possibilities. A daring quartet of prisoners managed to fake up a key to the SS clothing store and on 20 June 1942, dressed as two officers and two warrant officers, used another faked-up key to visit the arms store, stole a visiting officer's car, and drove away in it, being saluted smartly by the sentry, who did not bother to look at their forged passes. One of them, called Jaster, bore a report of Pilecki's which he delivered in Warsaw.[20] Rumour swelled their numbers; the incident greatly cheered the prisoners who remained behind. They had a few rough weapons ready enough to hand: pick helves, spades, hammers, mauls, hand axes, a few two-handed felling axes: no use against an alert sub-machine-gunner, but not perfectly useless in a scrimmage or at night.

One or two attempts at mass break-outs were made with these hand weapons, all with ill result though nine men out of one party of fifty did get clean away, and altogether over six hundred prisoners escaped, one way or another. Over half of these six hundred were soon recaptured, humiliated and murdered.

Himmler himself visited the complex on 17–18 June 1942, watched a party of Jews arrive at Birkenau, saw most of them gassed, inspected the artificial-rubber works run in Auschwitz town by camp labour, asked to watch a woman being flogged, promoted Hoess a rank and went away.

Pilecki by now had four battalions of followers organized, about 500 of whom knew him by sight and name as a secret camp resistance leader: the secret was becoming much too open for safety. He had a fairly settled job, so far as anything in Auschwitz was settled, in the tailor's shop and all his 500 friends were vigilantly on the watch for Gestapo informers, of whom there were many. He began to feel uneasy; before he left, he had one more macabre task to carry through.

The SS had a weakness for black pullovers, which they had knitted for them by women prisoners. There were quite a lot of women in Auschwitz, and hundreds of thousands died in Birkenau, which was primarily a women's camp; endless opportunities for intrigue, corruption and romance resulted. Hoess himself had a prisoner mistress, as well as his own wife and children living with him just outside the main gate; this piece of misconduct was widely enough known for him to have no hold over the misdemeanours of his own men.

Pilecki's organization exploited the double SS weakness, for pretty girls and for warm clothes, and with the help of their hospital friends occasionally supplied the SS with pullovers or greatcoats bearing typhus-infected lice. A very few SS died as a result.

More direct action could be taken by men who had tired of life. At Sobibor camp, near Lublin, the *Sonderkommando* of about 300 men in the innermost camp decided to break out. SS men visited the tailor's shop, one by one,[21] to collect uniforms they had left there for pressing before they went on leave. A prisoner stood behind the shop door with a spade, and hit each SS man as hard as he could on the back of the head. When the tailors had collected fifteen corpses, and a pistol from each, the whole squad rushed the gate of the inner compound, got to the main gate, calling for others to join them, rushed that too and were out in the open. Half of them were brought back by the surrounding peasantry, because they were Jews. A few got away.[22] Himmler was so put out he had the whole camp closed down.

This escape was not till 14 October 1943, by which time Pilecki was well away from Auschwitz.

His escape was straightforward. He decided to leave in the spring of 1943, for another body of four escapers from Auschwitz, who had got out on the previous 29 December, included a dentist called Kuczbara who knew only too much about him, and had fallen back into Gestapo hands on 20 March. So it was extra dangerous for him to stay, and he was anxious also to impress in person on his superiors in Warsaw the readiness of the camp to rise, and the need for some positive partisan demonstration to give it the signal to do so.

He handed over military command to Major Bończa, and all the innumerable details he carried in his head to Henryk Bartosiewicz – both were his friends – and was ready to leave. He secured – this was child's play to one by now so experienced underground – a forged pass to join the bakery squad; the bakery lay outside the wire. By now he had left the tailor's shop for the parcel office – the SS got parcels, though the prisoners did not – and he faked illness on Easter Saturday, 24 April, to get out of that. Hospital friends discharged him in time to join his bakery squad on the next Monday/Tuesday night – like Peulevé, he was supposed to have typhus, but in this case he was not really ill at all. The prisoner boss of the bakery group was bribed with a piece of chicken, and a friend in the locksmith's squad produced a key to the bakery door. Two companion bakers were to leave with him; all had plain clothes beneath their camp uniforms.

After several sweltering hours (Pilecki had never been in a bakery before), one of them cut the telephone wires, another unlocked the door, and at a moment when none of the SS was in sight they all went through it and ran.

It was a fine night for escape, dark and pouring with rain, and they got to the bank of the Vistula, several miles away, unchallenged. They had everything they needed except food. 'This had crossed their minds in the bakery, but at the last moment, in the heat of the dash for freedom, they had forgotten to get a few loaves.'[23] Pilecki moreover was racked by sciatica. Luck stayed with them: they found a dinghy on the river bank, padlocked, and by a miracle the bakery key opened the padlock.[24]

They hid in a wood all day on Tuesday, and in another wood farther east all Wednesday. Next night, with a priest's help, they crossed into the General Government, kept south of Cracow, and came on 2 May to a safe address in Bochnia, a town some twenty miles east of it. There Pilecki inquired for the nearest Home Army unit, and found it, by a singular freak, to be commanded by Tomasz Serafiński whose name he had been using in captivity.

Cracow District of the Home army could not be got to take any interest in Auschwitz. Pilecki persevered, and went to the main head-quarters in Warsaw. There they had 'a heap of files', with all his reports in them and others, but could not be persuaded that the risks of an action against it were worth the running. If ever there was a countrywide rising, he was assured, Auschwitz would not be forgotten; and that was all.[25]

He turned to other duties, fighting through the Warsaw rising of August–September 1944; survived even that catastrophe[26] and spent the rest of the war, under a different false identity, in a prisoner of war camp in Germany. Auschwitz had been an experience so shattering that he was looking for no more adventure; having lived through that and the Warsaw rising was, he felt, enough.

Or was it? When the Third Reich crumbled quite away, he moved southward in the crowds of what were pathetically named 'displaced persons', and reported to the Polish army in Italy. It was put to him that someone of his almost uncanny tenacity in adversity would be just the man to go back into Russian-occupied Poland on a mission for the Polish government in exile in London.

He went; but Communist subterfuge surpassed even his own. He was arrested almost immediately he arrived; who betrayed him has never been cleared up. In 1948 he was executed; no one outside the Polish and Russian secret police forces is quite sure when, or where. His wife and daughter, who survived him in Poland, were not even told where he is buried.

8

Conclusion

The six central characters in this book, each an example of resisters' courage in action, have points in common as well as obvious differences. Four men, two women; four of the six, parents; five of the six, married – and in four cases out of those five, divorced also. (Is there a study waiting to be done on the impact of military tension on marital happiness?) Even in this narrow sample, they spread in their class origins from two grandsons of peasants to the granddaughter of a marquise. It would be absurd to think of placing them in any order of merit; almost as absurd, to try to range them in any political order from right to left.

'Left' and 'right' are not in any case terms charged with much meaning, in the context of resistance to foreign occupation or Nazi tyranny. A Loustaunau-Lacau, though a far right-winger in French politics, was as good and as determined a resister as a Malraux or a Tillon on the opposite wing. Marie-Madeleine Fourcade with her aristocratic connections was just as firmly anti-Nazi as Harry Peulevé, with his friends in the *Franc-tireurs et partisans*, or Witold Pilecki cooperating with Cyrankiewicz in Auschwitz. Jean Moulin the administrator worked hand in glove – though also in friendly rivalry – with Pierre Brossolette the Socialist; both could put their knees under the same committee table with Fernand Grenier or Kriegel-Valrimont who were Communists.

It is just worth a glance at how that uncertain stream, the shower of official decorations, played over the half-dozen at whose careers we have looked. Moulin, as Caporal Mercier, received from the hands of General de Gaulle – both near tears – the Croix de la Libération, during his visit to England between his two missions. Marie-Madeleine Fourcade held the proper rank in the Legion of Honour, was an OBE, and had the French and the Belgian Croix de Guerre. Harry Peulevé had the same French decorations as she did, as well as a Military Cross for his first mission and a DSO for his second. Victor Gerson was delighted to hear of George Levin's DSO, and was somewhat surprised to be himself appointed OBE (Civil) instead. Andrée de Jongh was awarded a George Medal, as were several of her 'Comet' colleagues, and much more lately has had the distinction of being advanced to the high social rank of countess. Witold Pilecki, not the least brave even in this company, received no decoration at all while he was alive; ultimately, the Polish Republic awarded him the *Virtuti Militari*, the highest national gallantry award, first established by an eighteenth-century King of Poland.

What the six people round whom this book is built had in common, beyond their manifest bravery, was a particular strand in it of extra toughness; toughness a good way beyond the common run. In Pilecki's case, so daring – at first glance, to the point of absurdity – were his notions of how to resist, that it might even be thought he had a death wish. If he did, he received it; but there is no need to be so stern in assessing him. He was just, even for a Pole, quite remarkably tough.

His courage had something in it of the quality of the commando captain, P.A. Porteous, who strolled up to a German medium battery during the Dieppe raid, asked to speak to the battery commander, and persuaded him to surrender instead of waiting to be massacred; and got a well deserved Victoria Cross for the exploit. But it had something more as well.

All these six possessed long-term as well as short-term courage: not only the nerve that sustains a commando through a raid, or a sailor through a night's sea battle, or an airman through a fourteen-hour transcontinental sortie, or even a soldier through a week's continuous bombardment and close combat, but something more. They had an inner strength that went on, and on, and on, and on,

128

for months and even years; lived the width of a razor's edge from perdition.

Whence people get this strength is a question for the moralist or the psychologist, rather than the historian. Neither morality, nor psychology, nor political theory can be divorced wholly from fact. When people try to apply any abstract doctrine to human affairs, regardless of consequences, the consequences are apt to be frightful. Consider what happened when Hitler, Himmler and Rosenberg had scope to apply their doctrines in eastern Europe; not to speak of some later examples, almost as distressing.

This is a history book, not a tract; but it cannot end without raising one or two questions about how people behave, and ought to behave. What ought an old resister, or come to that a new one, to feel about new tyrannies? A Jean Moulin did not die, silent; a Harry Peulevé or a Marie-Madeleine Fourcade did not escape; an Andrée de Jongh, a Victor Gerson, a Witold Pilecki did not help others to escape; to enable one iron regime to replace another. Few, if any, resisters put up with what they went through, simply for that.

We can remain astonished at the paradox that the world's freedom from Nazism was in large part secured by Lavrenti Beria, the head of Stalin's NKVD, which terrorized from behind the armed forces of the USSR that played a cardinal part in the Allied victory against Hitler. Beria did not long survive Stalin, but the regime that followed those two ogres was not one that loved liberty.

At the end of the 1980s, the citizens of the USSR at last broke it up, into several component republics, doing their best to dispose of the police tyranny that it had become; yet though the NKVD's successor, the KGB, has been dissolved, many of its former members still turn up on the diplomatic lists of the successor states. The old saying that the price of liberty is eternal vigilance has lost no force with time. Other tyrannies have left their black marks on recent history in other places; the need to resist them does not die away.

None of the six principal resisters in this book could act alone; this deserves emphasis. They were sometimes exceedingly lonely: Moulin, for example, at the moment of his attempted suicide, or

Pilecki on the damp floor of the riding school at the moment of his first arrest. But to get anything – or anything beyond self-killing – done, anything that would make a proper dent in the occupation machine, they all had to have companions: everyone did. Those who were still alive when I first wrote this book only agreed to appear in it at all, on condition it stated somewhere how much they depended on their helpers and colleagues.

Readers will have noticed already how much this was so. Moulin by himself could have done little; with the help of the native-born French movements on one side of the channel, and the signals and supply resources of SOE and the RAF on the other, he could do a great deal. 'Poz 55', gallant as she was, depended on the leadership of Loustaunau-Lacau and Faye, of 'Saluki' and 'Grand Duke'; on the technical skills of her hundreds of informants and on the simple bravery of a 'Dromedary' and a 'Flying Fish'. Without Arnold Deppé, Andrée de Jongh's line would never have begun; without dozens of others, 'Tante Go', 'Michou', her own father and Florentino Giocoechea above all, it could never have continued. Victor Gerson's lines depended quite as much on many couriers and safe-house-keepers as they did on mountain guides or on himself. Harry Peulevé's strong circuit in the Corrèze and the Dordogne owed much to SOE and to the RAF; more to the stern will of the inhabitants of the Corrèze and the Dordogne to have done with the Nazis. He could never have got out of Buchenwald without the willing help of a large number of his fellow-captives. And Pilecki's organization inside Auschwitz depended entirely on trust: trust between companions in misfortune; trust that was sometimes betrayed, but generally held, and held fast.

A large proportion of these colleagues-in-arms, in all six of these cases, were chance-met and before the call came to them to resist, were more or less ordinary people pursuing more or less ordinary lives (there are ordinary counts, as well as ordinary railway porters; ordinary pilots, as well as ordinary schoolmasters). Plain straightforward men and women, who happened to have a particular kind of fire burning inside them – 'principle can dwell in a man like fire in a flint', as Mr Gladstone once put it – turned out able to go through a surprising number of twists and turns, when they had to, and to win victories that plain straightforward generals could not encompass.

What was this inner fire that made plain people do such extraordinary things, when suddenly put to the test? It was composed of several ways of feeling, some of them now out of fashion: patriotism, for example, which Edith Cavell reminded us is 'not enough', and which people who have never realized that their own country is in danger may never themselves have felt. Courage, loyalty, character, determination, will; they may be old-fashioned or unfashionable virtues, must they become empty words? On the contrary, in a soft capitalist world under threat from a fresh outbreak of Muslim terror, the need for them is as great as it was sixty years ago.

The readiness to resist was not confined to grown-ups. Here, in a final anecdote, is an example from the fringe of the great 'Prosper' disaster of the summer of 1943, the body blow to the section of SOE that Peulevé worked in, which coincided in time with Moulin's arrest. These are survivors, still in action a year later. The scene lies south of Paris and east of Orleans; there have been dozens of alarms, arrests, skirmishes over the past few days, as the German army wrestles with insubordinate rear areas while it tries to check the main flood of invasion in Normandy.

On 4 August, Monsieur and Madame Corjon were taken at six in the evening from the Château des Praslins to the *Feldkommandantur* at Montargis, with their comrades arrested at Dammarie-sur-Loing. As they left Les Praslins, Monsieur Corjon bade his daughter farewell, and gave her a final message for his comrades in arms: 'Tell them all, darling, that I did my duty as a Frenchman and that I said nothing.'

At her father's request, Mademoiselle Corjon went to ask Monsieur Carrier, of her father's group, to destroy a marked map and a message, which might have compromised the Resistance. Then she went to Bellevue [a nearby farm]. The Germans were still there. Without troubling about the risk, she went alone into the kitchen and took from the maquis letter-box – a covered sugar-bowl on the dresser – a message in clear which had been got ready for the messenger from Saint-Firmin, due in the day before. She popped the message in her mouth and swallowed it; the Germans noticed nothing. She was twelve years old.[1]

These people valued things of flesh and blood, the individuality and the dignity of human beings, above political doctrines and political machines; they were human themselves, not automata. What disgusted them about Nazism, besides its foreign-ness and its cruelty, was its inhumanity, its soullessness, its enmity for anything lively, fresh and original in the countries the Nazis conquered.

These six, at least, among the millions of Europeans who lived under the occupier's yoke in the last great European civil war, and dreamed of a new and less tyrannical Europe that might rise out of the ashes, were not cowards and they were not mean. If a single word can encompass what they had in them that made their courage so special, that word is integrity.

Chapter Notes

Chapter One

1   In a letter to Churchill, 7 November 1944, in Chaim Weizmann, *Trial and Error* (Hamish Hamilton 1949), p.537. Books in English were published in London, books in French in Paris, unless another place is given.

2   R. Harris Smith, *OSS* (University of California Press 1972), pp.332–3.

3   Cape 1935.

4   Cape 1940.

5   For further discussion of resisters' characteristics see M.R.D. Foot, *Resistance* (Eyre Methuen 1976), ch 2.

6   R.V. Jones, *Most Secret War* (Hamish Hamilton 1978), pp.349–50.

7   On the work of these light aircraft, see Hugh Verity, *We Landed by Moonlight* (Wilmslow: Air Data Publications, 1994), and his article, 'Some RAF Pick-ups for French Intelligence' in K.G. Robertson ed. *War, Resistance and Intelligence* (Barnsley: Leo Cooper, 1999), pp.169–84.

8   Pages 42–9, 57, 65.

9   Sir J.C. Masterman, *The Double-Cross System In the War of 1939 to 1945* (Yale University Press 1972, Granada 1979), a masterly survey written at the end of the war by the officer in charge of the details at the time: and R.F. Hesketh, *Fortitude* (St Ermin's Press 1999), written in 1945–8 by the officer in charge of the main deception plan, of which the codeword gave him his title.

10   See Ronald Lewin, *Ultra Goes to War* (Hutchinson 1978) and

(Sir) F.H. Hinsley et al., *British Strategic Intelligence in the Second World War*, first three vols (in four parts), (HMSO 1979–88).

11 David Kahn, *The Codebreakers* (2 ed., New York: Scribners 1986), pp.595–601.

12 D.H. McLachlan, *Room 39* (Weidenfeld & Nicolson 1968) and A.W. Dulles, *The Craft of Intelligence* (New York: New American Library, 1965) are the best 'pre-Ultra' general surveys. McLachlan throws out hints, that users of 'Ultras' will have picked up, about how useful it was. Patrick Beesly, *Very Special Intelligence* (Hamish Hamilton 1977) on the naval, and R.V. Jones *Most Secret War* on the air struggle are highly informative. Abram N. Shulsky, *Silent War* (New York: Brassey's (US) 1991) is suggestive. And on defectors, Christopher Andrew and Oleg Gordievsky, *KGB* (Hodder and Stoughton 1990) and Christopher Andrew and Vasili Mitrokhin, *The Mitrokhin Archive* (Allen Lane 1999) are valuable.

13 A.J. Evans, *The Escaping Club* (The Bodley Head 1921) repays study.

14 Chapters 5, 6 and 7.

15 Anne Frank's *Het Achterhuis* (Amsterdam: Contact 1957), often translated, has now been authenticated by a parallel-text edition of its various versions: D. Barnouw and G. van der Strom eds. *The Diary of Anne Frank* (Viking 1989).

16 H. Kühnrich, *Der Partisanenkrieg* (Berlin: Dietz 1968) is the only full study from outside the Soviet umbrella, and it has enormous gaps.

17 P. Trouillé, *Journal d'un Préfet pendant l'Occupation* (Gallimard 1964), pp.201–4.

Chapter Two

1 There are several lives of Moulin: H. Michel, *Jean Moulin l'unificateur* (Hachette 1964), his sister Laure Moulin, *Jean Moulin* (Presses de la Cité 1969), and an enormous life by

Daniel Cordier, who was close to him for most of the last year of his life – three volumes out of a projected six have so far appeared: *Jean Moulin l'inconnu du Panthéon* (J.-C. Lattès, 1989–93). Cordier has also written *La République des Catacombes* (Gallimard 1999), which covers much of the ground – to the end. In English, there is an essay by Eric Piquet-Wicks in *Four in the Shadows* (Jarrolds 1957), pp.31–100, based on personal knowledge and recollection, not on documents. Patrick Marnham, *The Death of Jean Moulin* (John Murray 2000) takes a less favourable view, even doubting the suicide attempt.

2   1m 70cm (5ft 7ins): tall men such as de Gaulle or Dewavrin therefore called him short.

3   J.E. Haynes and H. Klehr, *Venona* (Yale UP 1999), pp.211–2. Robert Conquest, *The Great Terror* (Penguin 1971), Roy Medvedev, *Let History Judge* (Oxford UP 1989) and Christopher Andrew and Oleg Gordievsky, *KGB* are still the best guides to the Soviet secret services.

4   His own account of these few days at Chartres can be found in his *Premier Combat*, notes written for his sister next winter and published by her in Paris in 1946.

5   He was *mis en disponibilité* – put on half pay. In July 1942 he was placed on retired pay, by a regime that had lost direct touch with him.

6   Moulin had one Jewish connection, a half-Jewish step-grand-mother. This did not bring him within the scope of the Nazis', or of Vichy's, racial 'purity' laws.

7   Moulin's report – clearly written by a civil servant, not by a Communist – is given in full in M.R.D. Foot, *SOE in France* (HMSO 1968), pp.489–98, in an English translation made at the time. His sister re-translated it into French in her life of him. The original, then mislaid, has been rediscovered, and awaits publication when the French translation of *SOE in France*, now under clearance in a new edition, appears.

8   1958, in Laure Moulin, *Jean Moulin*, p.260, tr.

9   The early members of de Gaulle's secret staffs took as

their pseudonyms the names of Paris Métro stations. J-L. Crémieux-Brilhac, *Colonel Passy* (Odile Jacob 2000) collects into one volume, with introduction and notes, Dewavrin's three volumes of war memoirs, dating from 1947–51.

10 See Foot, *SOE in France*, p. 83.

11 Details in Foot, *Resistance*, ch. v.

12 See H.R. Kedward, *Resistance in Vichy France* (Oxford UP 1978), ch. vii.

13 This was General de Lattre de Tassigny, who escaped, and was flown out to join de Gaulle by Hugh Verity from a secret landing-ground in Burgundy in September 1943.

14 R. Hostache, *Le Conseil National de la Résistance* (Presses Universitaires de France, 1958).

15 See Mark Seaman, *Bravest of the Brave* (Michael O'Mara 1997).

16 See G. Brossolette, *Il s'appelait Pierre Brossolette* (Albin Michel 1976), by his widow, and G. Piketty, *Pierre Brossolette* (Odile Jacob, 1998), his son-in-law, both full of detail, the latter also full of scholarly references. Piquet-Wicks also discusses him, in *Four in the Shadows*, p.169ff.

17 The owner of the house, and both the secretaries of the committee, had been members with Moulin of Pierre Cot's *cabinet* before the war.

18 After the war, the French security services tracked Barbie down to an address in Westphalia, from which they could not persuade the Americans to extradite him. He later fled to South America, and was eventually brought back to France for trial, sentenced to life imprisonment in 1987 and died in prison in Lyons four years later.

19 Laure Moulin, *Jean Moulin*, p.12, tr.

Chapter Three

1 Brian Crozier, *De Gaulle* (Eyre Methuen, 2v 1973), i.37.

2 M.-M. Fourcade, tr. Kenneth Morgan, *Noah's Ark* (Allen & Unwin 1973), p.26.

3   ibid. pp.48–9.

4   ibid. p.332.

6   ibid. pp.154, 126.

6   ibid. p.203.

7   ibid. p.232.

8   ibid. pp.244, 237.

9   See K.G. Robertson ed. *War, Resistance and Intelligence* (Leo Cooper 1999), p.181.

10   *Noah's Ark*, p.255.

11   ibid. p.362.

12   ibid. p.267.

Chapter Four

1   *Foreign Office List* (1924), p.327.

2   So far, this chapter rests on his family papers, kindly made available by his sister.

3   See pages 27–8.

4   See Foot, *SOE in France*, p.9.

5   Details ibid., pp.53–9, and in C. Cunningham, *Beaulieu* (Leo Cooper 1998).

6   When a uniformed prisoner of war in the autumn of 1944, I took care to conceal from the Germans the fact that I spoke German; but, delirious in a German military hospital after severe wounds incurred during an unsuccessful escape, for some days talked nothing else.

7   For his adventures in Bordeaux, and later in Normandy – both extensive – see Foot, *SOE in France*, pp.277–81, 408–9, etc. He died just before Christmas 1974 (*Times* obituary 7 January 1975).

8   Poirier's *The Giraffe has a long Neck* (Leo Cooper 1992) is invaluable for the next six paragraphs, and for pages 64–70.

9   1961–70 supplement (Oxford UP 1981), p.841a.

10   Denis Rake, *Rake's Progress* (Leslie Frewin 1968), p.190.

11 Quoted by (Sir) B.H. Liddell Hart in *Great Contemporaries: Essays by Various Hands* (Cassell 1935), pp.216–7.

12 She starred, in her middle nineties, in a television programme, 'The Real Charlotte Grays', in February 2002.

13 Both are now said to be dead. Déricourt's case, once a great newspaper sensation, is examined in some detail in Foot, *SOE in France*, ch. x.

14 Conversation with H.M.R. Despaigne, an agent who travelled in the other aircraft, October 1975. See Hugh Verity, *We Landed by Moonlight* (Ian Allan 1978), p.121.

15 Conversation with an eyewitness, 1969.

16 Foot, *SOE in France*, p.421.

17 For details of arms drops, types of aircraft load etc., see ibid. appx C. For arms sent to France, see Pierre Lorain, ed. and tr. David Kahn, *Secret Warfare* (Orbis 1983), unofficial but admirable.

18 Olivier Todd, *André Malraux* (Gallimard 2001) is sceptical about his hero's resistance activities.

19 Hiller died young (*Times* obituary 27 November 1972), of muscular dystrophy, ending prematurely a successful career as a diplomat; Watney is still alive.

20 B.H. Cowburn, *No Cloak, No Dagger* (Jarrolds 1960), ch x, gives a vivid account of exactly what it felt like to do this.

21 See *The Giraffe has a Long Neck*, pp.83–5.

22 See profile of the Abbé in *Observer*, 30 August 1953.

23 See his *Journal d'un Préfet pendant l'Occupation* (Gallimard 1964), *passim*.

24 Eugen Kogon, *Der SS-Staat* (Stockholm: Hermann-Fischer 1947). Dr Kogon was less fortunate in the title of his English translation, *The Theory and Practice of Hell* (1950); the book is nevertheless terrifying and impressive.

25 H. Krausnick and others, *The Anatomy of the SS State* (1968), particularly pages 397–504 by Martin Broszat.

26 See Mark Seaman, *Bravest of the Brave* (Michael O'Mara 1997).

27 Conversation with Balachowsky, who because he was a

scientist – he was an entomologist – had been enrolled in Block 50; 1969.

28 Where other sources are not stated, this chapter rests on distant recollections of his SOE file, on *DNB*, on his family papers, and on conversations with a few close friends of his in the mid-1970s.

Chapter Five

1 See Bickham Sweet-Escott, *Baker Street Irregular* (Methuen 1965), chs i and ii, and obituary of L.D. Grand who ran it in *The Times*, 5 December 1975.

2 Foot, *SOE in France*, 156, 161–3. This chapter otherwise rests on recollections of the Gersons' SOE files – which will go public shortly at the Public Record Office – and on several talks with him, mainly in 1969.

3 One member of this committee, called in SOE's files 'Maximence', took a lot of tracing. The codename turned out to be simply an Englishman's mishearing of his name, Max Hymans, a retired politician, with whom SOE had got in touch through Thomas Cadett, previously the BBC's man in Paris. Cadett did a lot for F section in its early days, though he never headed it; he moved over to political warfare, on a disagreement with his SOE superiors, in the winter of 1941–2.

4 Robert O. Paxton, *Vichy France* (New York: Norton, 1972), pp.181–5, gives further references. There was a prolonged press sensation on this subject in France in the early 1990s.

5 Frequently mentioned in her *Service d'Evasion*: which with Jean-Pierre Bloch (to whom we come in a moment) *Le Vent souffle sur l'Histoire* (1956) provides most of the accounts of the 'Vic' line in print.

6 Quoted from Foot, *SOE in France*, p.97.

7 Cape 1941.

8 Photographs of both – Lyon called 'Acolyte', his codename – in Foot, *SOE in France*, after p.196.

9   His *Knights of the Floating Silk* (Hutchinson 1959), pp.160–73, covers the escape.

10 It did not make testing them easy that DF sent in by parachute, as a guinea pig, a young American who was both a heavy drinker and addicted to pretty girls.

11 Conversation with him, 1966.

12 H.J. Giskes, *London calling North Pole* (Kimber 1953) explains how he did it. Pieter Dourlein, *Inside North Pole* (same), describes what his victims felt like. M.R.D. Foot, *SOE in the Low Countries* (St Ermin's Press 2001) explains what went wrong at the London end.

13 Sir J.C. Masterman, *The Double-Cross System in the War of 1939–1945* (Yale UP 1972), an almost complete account by the man who supervised much of the detail, and Sir Michael Howard, *Strategic Deception* (HMSO 1990), the fifth volume in Sir F.H. Hinsley's series on *British Intelligence in the Second World War*, are between them decisive.

14 Foot, *SOE in France*, pp.312–4.

Chapter Six

1   Paul Routledge, *Public Servant, Secret Agent* (Fourth Estate 2002), a life of Airey Neave, p.127.

2   These four famous words were added in 1924 to the following sentence (which there reads 'for' instead of 'towards') on the plinth of Frampton's statue of her outside the National Portrait Gallery, near Trafalgar Square. See the life of her by Rowland Ryder (1975), pp.214, 237.

3   *Father Damien: an open letter to the Reverend Dr Hyde of Honolulu* (Chatto & Windus 1890). Stevenson's very different *Dr Jekyll and Mr Hyde* had appeared four years before; otherwise, it would have been quite easy to guess where the villain's name came from. The rumour that Stevenson recanted is quite untrue.

4   Airey Neave's life of her, with this title (Hodder and Stoughton

1954), still holds the field.

5   Ryder, *Edith Cavell*, p.236.

6   J.M. Langley, *Fight Another Day* (Collins 1974), p.167.

7   Colonel Rémy, *Réseau Comète* (Perrin 1966), i.30, much the fullest account of the line in print; my translation.

8   ibid. i.45.

9   Airey Neave, *Saturday at MI9* (Hodder and Stoughton 1969), p.133.

10 Though Valenciennes was in France, not Belgium, it lay in one of the two French departments – the Nord and the Pas-de-Calais – which the Germans found it more convenient to administer from Brussels than from Paris. In fact, by the time she got this far, she was already within the Brussels Gestapo's orbit, though she still had the frontier to cross.

11 Known for some obscure reason during the war as an 'escapee'; but we do not need to adopt wartime bureaucrats' bad grammar.

12 Neave could only call him 'Monday'; Langley, *Fight Another Day*, p.167, gave his name; *Who was who 1981–90* (Black 1991), p.171, gives his later ambassadorial career and his knighthood. He died in 1986.

13 *Saturday at MI9*, p.143.

14 ibid. p.142.

15 ibid. pp.131, 157.

16 ibid. pp.158–9.

17 See Foot, *SOE in the Low Countries*, pp.251–4.

18 Rémy, i.81, tr.

19 Jimmy Langley met the aircraft that brought Peggy van Lier to England from Iberia, was greatly struck by her, and married her soon afterwards.

Chapter Seven

1   Reuben Ainsztein, *Jewish Resistance in Nazi-occupied Eastern Europe* (Elek 1974), p.183; a devastating book.

2   Examples in Madeleine Masson, *Christine* (Hamish Hamilton

1975) – her heroine 'Christine Granville's' mother was the daughter of a Jewish banker, and married to a count; and in Julia Namier, *Lewis Namier* (Oxford UP 1971) – Lady Namier's second husband the historian, descended from a very learned Jewish family, was the son of a Galician landowner.

3   Ainsztein, op. cit., pp.217, 233.

4   Jozef Garliński, *Fighting Auschwitz* (Friedman 1975), p.14. I am greatly indebted to this book and to its author.

5   (Sir) Peter Wilkinson and Joan Bright Astley, *Gubbins and SOE* (Leo Cooper 1993), p.36.

6   There were Poles, it is true, who were ready to work with the Russian enemy; but for political reasons, because they were Socialists or Communists, not to get rich themselves.

7   The best account of Polish resistance in English is Jozef Garliński's *Poland, SOE and the Allies* (Allen and Unwin 1969).

8   For its legal status, see M. Ney-Krwawicz, *The Polish Resistance Home Army 1939–1945* (Hammersmith: Polish Underground Movement Study Trust, 2001).

9   At a conference in Oxford in 1962.

10   Christopher Andrew and Oleg Gordievsky, *KGB* (Hodder and Stoughton 1990), p.540.

11   Garliński's tr.: *Fighting Auschwitz*, p.20.

12   Its name, *Schutzstaffel*, simply means protection squad.

13   George H. Stein, *The Waffen-SS* (Columbia University Press 1966) remains authoritative.

14   Garliński's tr.: *Fighting Auschwitz*, p.32, from Hoess's own account.

15   ibid. pp.260–2.

16   ibid. pp.244–5.

17   ibid. p.257.

18   See Nicholas Bethell, *The Last Secret* (Deutsch 1974).

19   Example in Garliński, *Fighting Auschwitz*, p.113.

20   ibid. pp.102–3, 271–3.

21   The tailor's shop at Auschwitz was not part of the *Sonderkommando*: at Sobibor it was.

22 Ainsztein, *Jewish Resistance*, pp.759–69.
23 Garliński, *Fighting Auschwitz*, p.170.
24 Another good Catholic, fleeing from a much milder enemy, had encountered a similar miracle with a padlock: Eamon De Valera escaping from Lincoln gaol in February 1919.
25 Garliński, *Fighting Auschwitz*, pp.173–4.
26 See J. M. Ciechanowski, *The Warsaw Rising of 1944* (Cambridge UP 1974), the best account.

Chapter Eight

1 Paul Guillaume, *Au Temps de l'Héroisme et de la Trahison* (Orleans: Imprimerie Nouvelle, 1948), p.290, tr.

Note on Books

There is already an immense popular and semi-popular literature on resistance in the war of 1939–45 and plodding, scholarly studies appear in English as well, as the subject has now become one for doctoral theses. Unfortunately, as so often happens, the scholars turn up their noses at the popular books, as unreliable or downright misleading, and too many learned authors write unappetizing prose. One of the profoundest of them, himself a writer of real grace and power, once even ventured from Paris the opinion that, where English books on resistance are concerned, a foreigner cannot tell where the historian lays down the pen and the novelist picks it up.[1]

To see where resistance fits into the history of the rest of the war, the reader can pursue the references to it in Peter Calvocoressi, Guy Wint and John Pritchard, *The Penguin History of the Second World War* (new ed. 1999); or Henri Michel, *The Second World War* (Deutsch 1975, translated from the Paris version of 1968); or I.C.B. Dear and M.R.D. Foot eds. *The Oxford Companion to World War II*, 2 ed. (Oxford University Press 2001).

There are two brief outline histories of resistance in French, Michel's *Les Mouvements Clandestins en Europe* (Presses Universitaires de France 1961) and Henri Bernard's *Histoire de la Résistance Européenne* (Verviers: Marabout Université 1968). Fuller studies are Michel's *The Shadow War*, tr. R. H. Barry (Deutsch 1972), my own *Resistance* (Eyre Methuen 1976, Paladin 1978), and Jorgen Haestrup, *Europe Ablaze* (Odense: University

---

[1] Henri Michel, *Bibliographie critique de la Résistance* (Institut Pédagogique National 1964), p.84.

Press 1978). On particular aspects of resistance, a few books are worth mention:

On intelligence:

> D.H. McLachlan, *Room 39* (Weidenfeld & Nicolson 1968)
> R.V. Jones, *Most Secret War* (Hamish Hamilton 1978) and *Reflections on Intelligence* (Heinemann 1989)
> F.H. Hinsley and others, *British Strategic Intelligence in the Second World War*, (HMSO 1979–90)
> Abram N. Shulsky, *Silent Warfare* (New York: Brassey's (US), 1991)

On escape:

> A.J. Evans, *The Escaping Club* (Bodley Head 1921, Panther 1957)
> Airey Neave, *Saturday at MI9* (Hodder and Stoughton 1969)
> M.R.D. Foot and J.M. Langley, *MI9* (Boston: Little, Brown 1980)

On subversion:

> Curzio Malaparte, *La technique du coup d'état* (Grasset 1931)
> Bickham Sweet-Escott, *Baker Street Irregular* (Methuen 1965)
> R. Harris Smith, *OSS* (Berkeley: University of California Press 1972)
> M.R.D. Foot, *SOE: an outline history 1940–1946* (new ed. Pimlico 1999)